Challenges of an Aircraft Photographer

Rev 7 Sept. 2012

Richard Young
Copyright 2012

Econohost Publishing

Preface

Photography is a field that just started to take off about 100 years ago and what you would see in films was captured live with very limited post effects.

Although special challenges and camera techniques were intimidating at times, problem solving for photography has not changed.

I found out early in my career that it was essential to use technology to get the shots that I imagined.

Contained in the pages of this autobiography are some of the challenges I faced while doing air to air photography. Throughout the book are listed the techniques and hardware that I used to "Capture the Shots".

During this time there were no computer graphics and special effects were limited to optical effects that were only used in transitions and titles.

If technology failed, we used "Gaffers Tape" and lots of it.

Digital photography makes "snap shots" easy, but going "Totally manual" is the only way to make your photography "Your Art".

Technology aside, Industrial Photography is basically the very old art of telling stories, but now we tell stories with still and moving pictures. In any case, your story will have to "stand the test of time" to be a successful story teller.

I will try to explain how I applied these rules in aerial photography. This book should prove to be interesting even for the seasoned professional.

TOC

Preface

TOC

"Discover Flying" On a Shoestring
   Studio Shoot For Master Shots
   Watching Them Squirm in Ponca City
   Technical Notes "Discover Flying" On a Shoestring

The 99"s Still Event Shoot
   Production Notes "99"s Still Documentary Shoot"

Setting the Stage for Wide open Creativity

"I Think This Is the Beginning of a Beautiful Friendship"

Growing our Production Team
   Shooting Styles
   Two Contradictory Ways to Make a Movie

"The Incomparable Baron" – Flirting With Danger
   Location 1: Greensboro, NC:
   Location 2: Kitty Hawk, NC:
   The Camera work at Kitty Hawk:
   Production Notes At Kitty Hawk
   Location 3: Atlantic Ocean
   Location 4: Beech Mountain, NC
   Production Notes at Beech Mountain
   Movie Acceptance at the Annual Sales Show:

A Story of Cowboys and Airplanes
   The "New Pioneer" – Actor Rex Allen
   The "New Cowboy" from Costa Mesa
   The Quite Little West Texas Town of Lubbock
   My Time with the Cowboys
   The New Pioneer, The Rematch

Production Notes "The New Pioneer" A Story of
Cowboys and Airplanes

Before the "Predator" there was the "Streaker"
Production Notes "MQM107A" – "The Streaker"

AQM37C "Jayhawks" Never flew this Fast

How to Catch the Bad Guys, Use a Maritime Patrol
Aircraft
Correcting Color Problems

Can It Fly with Ice? The MU2
Production Notes for the MU2 Icing Tests

Extreme Environmental Flying
Change of Plans
Extreme Pain
New Shooting Technique
Money Shot in Trail

A Run-In with the US Government! "The Tradition
of Excellence"
How to get Pre Dawn Photos
Money shot at Mesa
The Bullfrog Basin Affair
Park Rangers Arrive
Production Notes "The Tradition of Excellence
1900C"

"Riding the Rocket Ship"
Production Notes "T-6A"

The Search for a Mystery Jet
Why the Search
Culture Shock Found In Japan
Mitsubishi Diamond Construction

The last flight of India Foxtrot Oscar 21
The Trip That Would Not End
Conspiracy – The investigation of an accident
Camera Location "CV"

The Accident
Stolen Equipment Dooms Aircraft!

The Secret Starship First Flight
 "Star" of the Show

"Starship Down"
 Starship Certified to Make History
 ASTROVISION by Clay Lacy
 VECTORVISION by Bob Nettmann
 SHOTMAKER by Hal Needham

Designing the Camera System

Beech Vision Shooting Strategies
 "Will Record"

Why our pilots were so good
 When we used "Other Pilots"
 Shooting Note: Propeller Planes and Library
 Archives

Making a Creative Video with NLE

How to stay away from the Feds
 Flying Low and Fast

Over Ambitious Photo Shoots

Engineering High Speed Tests
 High Speed Filming / Slow Motion

Terms and Specifications for Film Equipment
 Old School Photographer
 Film Processing System
 The 16mm Sound Transfer Process
 History of Double System Sound for Movies
 Film Stock
 Pushing Film
 Film – ECO 7252 EI 25
 Film – EF 7241 EI 160
 Film – VNF 7240 EI 400

The Telecine or Film Chain

Specifications for Airborne Video Equipment
Sony DXC-750 2/3" 3 Chip Power HAD – Camera
Outside Pan Tilt Hanging from Belly of Aircraft

Video Formats
PAL SECAM

I would like to thank the following for their contribution to this book.

"Discover Flying"

On a Shoestring

Location: Ponca City Ok. – 1969

This was my first movie and I was captivated with the whole process. The "camera", "speed", "action" thing was great. The talent was non-actors that the director found locally. One was a school teacher and one a flight instructor at the Beech dealership. Needles to say, each scene required many takes.

The acting was not natural. There was not a prompter in those days, but that was the quaint part of the movie because it was designed to show ordinary people taking flying lessons.

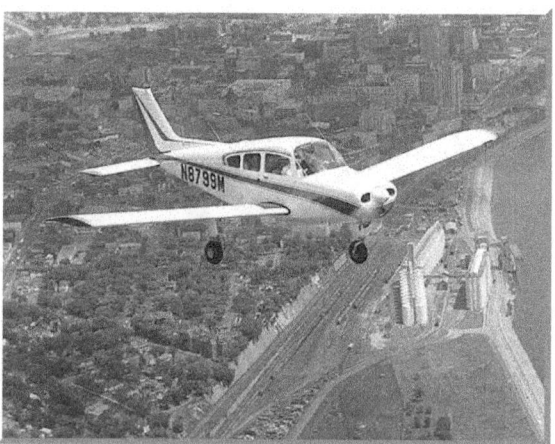

Model 23 Musketeer

Studio Shoot For Master Shots

There is not a human alive that does not make mistakes. To make a film or video you must have a

"Master shot" that close-ups can be cut too. Our master shot was in a large room where we could use a prompter to keep the narration flowing.

Using non-professional actors will increase the cost of your project period. They make more mistakes and as I found out, and they will not perform each take of a scene the same so you not only have to use cutaways more than necessary, you will find that matching action becomes a nightmare.

With non-professionals best to just give them an idea to get across and let them use their own words as the narration.

This technique has problems also, but you may have to try this method as a secondary way to get a scene if the scripted way is not working. Main troubles are that slang and grammar problems creep into the movie.

Watching Them Squirm in Ponca City

The director, besides his directing duties, would hold a reflector for lighting. As I remember, the poor actors were setting in a hot plane in July on the runway in Oklahoma. They took turns sweating and being blinded by the reflector. This shoot is where I learned all about how "cutaways" were used to break up a long dialogue and to cover for mistakes.

Technical Notes "Discover Flying" On a Shoestring

In retrospect we should have shot the school scene in a school location due to the lighting of the background as it did not look a classroom. Graphic animation along with original processing and work printing was accomplished at MPL in Memphis, Tennessee.

Prolonged outdoor shooting with talent should be limited to the early part of the day, if they are not comfortable the scene will look poor.

Process: Sound was laid off to the Magna Sync 16mm magnetic recorder as described later in this book. The Magna Sync looked like a 16mm system but the "film" was actually film stock with full covering of magnetic material instead of a light sensitive coating.

The 99"s Still Event Shoot

The Women Pilots" Organization Convention at Beech Field.

Much of what an Industrial Photographer will be asked to do is document events, portraits and candid shots to record the spontaneity of the event. Copy stand and Portrait Studio shooting can be mechanical due to subject matter and will not be covered in this book.

I was brand new to photography. The goal of this shoot was to document the events and provide some group setup shots. So, I just ran around shooting everything that look like it was important.

When the film was developed, I had a lot more shots than were necessary but as it turned out, the customer loved to have the coverage. This was film, so every time you pushed the button the cost increased, but we had a film lab in-house so film costs were not a factor. At the time film costs for B/W negative film ran about $2.00 a 36 exposure 35mm roll, processing was about $1.00 and a contact sheet about 75 cents.

The client was pleased and that is what you want if you are to get paid and get those return engagements.

Actually while I was shooting I was also doing a very important function for the shoot which is "Bracketing". Bracketing is not as important now days with the auto exposure cameras, however, sometimes if you can set your camera to "Manual" so you can bracket your shots. You might find interesting depth of field surprises as the background action becomes important or goes out of focus.

Also with the longer exposures a sense of action can be shown as some things will become "motion blurred". As a professional photographer of propeller driven aircraft the first thing you learned was using the slowest shutter speed produced the best pictures as the propeller became blurred and was not as important in the picture.

While the armature photographer used a high shutter speed to "Stop" the action and the propeller looked, being stopped, more like the World War II air to air shots. If you can control your camera with manual settings you have a much better chance of making a great shot.

Production Notes "99"s Still Documentary Shoot"

On this shoot all photos were hand held, with out a tripod for candid shots and tripod mounted (to reduce movement) for group shots. I used a 50mm lens on a Nikon SLR shooting negative 35mm print film. A few shots were from the top of a 75ft hanger capturing the participants with their airplanes in full frame, wing span of 60 feet. Always look for unusual angles and compositions. No sound, no reflectors or special filters, it was just "Run-N-Gun". If you have an assistant's help, you can get the names of people in each shot and maybe even do a quick and dirty supplemental lighting setup with reflectors. Note: I found that using a premade fold up silverside of a windshield shade worked great for a cheap reflector. One of these reflectors can be purchased at a department store for $5 or photo shop for $55.

Setting the Stage for Wide open Creativity

Things changed after I returned from a two year stint away from Beech. Gone were the Old AV Department and its entire roster of people. When I returned there was a new Cinematographer; Bob Braddy, who replaced the award winning photographer Luray Parker.

Luray went on to Wyoming and shot wildlife for the Wyoming Fish and Game Department until his recent retirement. The film director along with the manager, secretary, and audio man had also left the company or moved to other departments. Together with Bob, **we** now made the complete "Audio Visual Department" for Beech Aircraft.

Our department was spread over four offices areas all separated by stairs, but at least in one building. The AV / Sound department was accessed by going through the portrait studio then up three sets of stairs, across a catwalk and then into a storage room with limited ceiling height due to being just under the roof of a plant built in the 1930's.

Besides the noise from the film refrigerators, to keep the film cold, below my office was the machine shop. I had few visitors to my office due to its location. Bob's office was below mine, but it took almost 5 minutes to transverse the distance if we wanted to discuss a film. Even being in my mid 20's, that was O.K. but the stairs got old very fast.

"I Think This Is the Beginning of a Beautiful Friendship"

Bob was a photographer, not a sound tech. I initially had reservations about Bob but he turned out to be my best friend. We seemed to work together extremely well. A case in point is how we worked as a team on the "Incomparable Baron" project, our first film. We exchanged ideas and "Brainstormed" on projects using our own unique views.

Looking back on those first movies I think Bob was a lot smarter than I gave him credit. He was the visionary and I was the tech which is the perfect team. Even though our first movies were good and getting better and better. We were building a bond between us that made each movie more innovative than the last. If either of us had a problem with a shot we were quick to tell the other.

We got so good at producing a quality industrial film that people kept coming to us with new projects. Projects came from Marketing, Public Relations and Training requiring films both at the plant and at many locations around the U.S. At this time we started to coordinate with the photography department because it was more cost effective to shoot stills and movies at the same time.

Much later, I would be asked to do Litigation based video Reenactments with multi-millions of company dollars at stake.

Building a "niche" for your services builds longevity. In all videos that I made for litigation cases we had a 100% defense success rate. Many litigation shoots were to recreate conditions that at times I found were disturbing. I had to believe our test pilots knew what they were doing on flights, and that the accident was caused by something else.

Most of the "fun" shoots were for the Marketing department and required a different style of shooting. For Marketing, the story had to flow with a beginning, middle and end, telling the values of the product by building exciting scripting and visuals. Marketing videos and film can require creativity to pump up the story line.

Litigation documentation could not tolerate any creativity other than camera angles to better tell the story.

Growing our Production Team

It was about a year down the road when Bob hired another shooter because Bob, with his size, had problems with small spaces which also gave me the opportunity to learn how to shoot. I started shooting Air to Air in the back of small airplanes due to my light weight and small size.

The first air to air shoot was when Bob was flying the photo plane, Sundowner, and me in the back cargo area where I was shooting a Sierra in close formation over Monument Valley, one of my favorite places, located near the Four Corners area in south east Utah.

Monument Valley, on the ground, was used for such pictures as Forest Gump, Vacation, Back to the Future, and most of director John Ford's movies with John Wayne. I swear when I saw "Fort Apache", the Calvary was going on marches where they passed the same mountain that I remembered over and over again but from different directions.

Doug Ambler was hired as a film shooter in late 1973 and developed into a great photographer. He could be given any assignment knowing that he would bring back the film to tell the story.

I was already a pilot and Bob and Doug started to learn to fly, so that all three of us could communicate our requests to other pilots in there language. Doug Ambler is now in Kansas City the owner of "Mill Creek Woods Photography", when he is not being a professional pilot flying business jets.

About the same time we were growing our AV team, we also started incorporating the use of photographers from the still photography department for still shots when we had setup aircraft. Not only could they record images for use as still pictures but it gave us another body to use to help set up lighting, move gear when needed and on occasion even set in as a "model" or at least be a "stand in" until the real subject was needed.

Location shooting was easy and hard at times. We would setup a night shot where the aircraft would "Taxi" in from a landing and into a lighted ramp, stop its engines and then the models would deplane and walk into the Fixed Base Operators lobby. That shot would require maybe 5 takes to get all the people to be at and do the right thing to make the shot.

Now we add the aircraft operations, which had to have control tower coordination and we had to have both the camera and the sound ready for the shot.

Next the weather had to cooperate with low winds or the 2000 watt lights we strung around the ramp would blow over. A shot that would last 20 seconds on film may take three hours of prep and shooting to get in the can.

One night in Opa-Locka Florida we had one especially long day; the morning found us coordinating a four ship "air to air" from Opa-Locka over Miami and down the keys to an airport that is now a bunch of houses on Key Largo.

The formation shot took most of the day and we had scheduled a night shot at Opa-Locka with four models in evening attire. I don't remember if we had lunch or even dinner that day but we went on with the night shot. After lighting and shooting until about midnight, the crew looked at each other and passed when the models wanted to go to a night club to celebrate the shoot. Usually we would have jumped on the party wagon but this night we could barely get back to the hotel before we passed out from exhaustion.

Shooting Styles

Note: To this day I cannot stand the "hand held" shooting style that amateurs and some professional shooters use to pump up excitement in their films. To me, they use the hand held camera movement to "cover" shooting or a script's inadequacies.

As a shooter, I will turn off the show when they try this style, it makes me sick to watch if they overdue it. That said, sometimes the camera movement can be so slight that it does not distract from the story.

I see these tiny movements, but if it doesn't disturb the story plot I am happy. As a filmmaker I also see bad edits or jump cuts that are wrong, even lip sync that is off more than 1 frame is a sign of poor overdubbing. I have trained myself to see these problems in my films as I spot quality control problems, but it makes enjoyment of other films frustrating.

In marketing or commercial shooting you use a tripod or Steadicam for ALL SHOTS and you cannot go wrong.

Before the Steadicam we used DC powered gyros on "air to air" shots to reduce the bounces and bumps and we would use a dolly on moving shots on the ground.

Using a "Shoulder Pod" with our Arriflex "S" film camera was also vital when needed, but it required a camera man with total control of his breathing, as the shoulder pod used a support from the shooters chest. We could also use this with a 5.6mm lens on our 16mm cameras for ultra wide shots.

I used the 5.6mm when I was talked into setting in the co-pilots seat and shot the whole flight panel during aerobatics over the Pacific between Los Angles and Catalina Island.

Soon I would have to learn all parts of a camera and how to load, employ lighting and composition to accomplish a mission. I also familiarized myself with lighting and camera exposures for both time lapse, and high speed. All kinds of photography had a place in industrial photography and will be explained in later chapters.

Two Contradictory Ways to Make a Movie

1. Write a script, organize a budget, find talent, assemble a crew, direct, edit and distribute the production. (Very organized but hard to take advantage of "scenes of opportunity"). This style of production needs a person to follow shooting and check off shots when made and list what take was the good one.

2. Have outline of goals, and then couple them to a scenic location and brainstorm on location. Do what ever you

need to do to make the shots and finish the project. (Unorganized and much more fun)

On each film that I do, I submit a purposed budget for preplanning, shooting, and editing. If I overspend in one of those areas I have to make it up in another area or explain why there was an overrun.

Since this is not Hollywood the budget is really tight. Budgets were $1,000 a minute for films and dropped to $200 for videos. So shooting tape with a cost of $20 an hour was the least expensive thing, therefore, I shot allot and used just the best shots in the videos.

When doing formation work, I have been known to push record to start the tape and let it go until the tape runs out. Getting everyone to the position to shoot is the expensive part, tape is cheap, use it up. My MII would shoot for 90 minutes and not need a battery, which is about as long as you want to do air to air at one time. After that people tend to make poor decisions and can put themselves and the equipment in danger.

Note: Budgets for films and videos did not include airplane costs until companies found that charging against advertising moved the costs off the books, which really is where it should have been all along. When the charging changed, the budgets for marketing films skyrocketed.

"The Incomparable Baron" – Flirting With Danger

Locations – Greensboro and Kitty Hawk, NC – Myrtle Beach, SC & Beech Mountain, NC

I was being introduced to a new way of making a movie by Bob when we did the Baron movie. I can only say it was much more fun than having a finished script laid out before the first frame was shot. We found that the chemistry between us even became better as time went along.

Standing in the lobby of the Beech Dealership in Greensboro, NC looking at a picture of "The Wright Brothers First Flight at Kitty Hawk" hanging in all its glory. Bob and I talked about doing a location shoot at Kitty Hawk and as it turned out, this became the "Opening" of the film.

Location 1: Greensboro, NC:

On the first night at Greensboro, Dave Palay, the Baron pilot, found a couple of local models at the hotel and asked if they wanted to be in our movie. Well, we ended up taking them to Myrtle Beach for a shot on a boat.

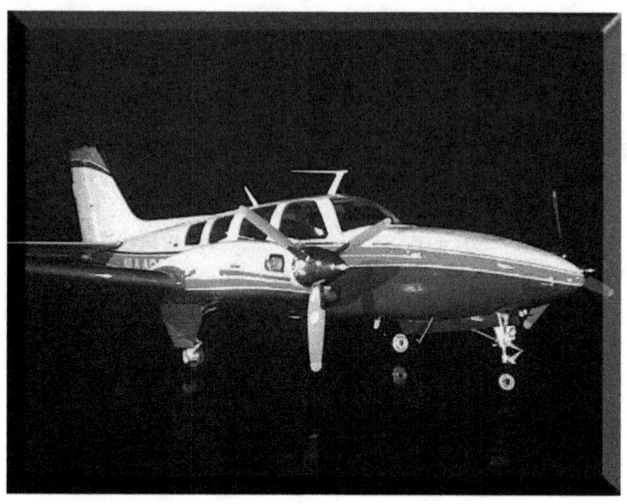

A lot of B-Roll extra shots including a night shot of the Baron on a watered down tarmac were completed at Greensboro. Another B-Roll shot of the instrument panel during the flight to the Kitty Hawk location and many shots of clouds going by filled other holes and allowed for cutaways.

Location 2: Kitty Hawk, NC:

If you are getting any ideas about how creativeness affects the story you are right. We did the "opening / money shot" at Kitty Hawk because I saw the beautiful painting in the lobby of the Beech dealership that showed the Kitty Hawk Monument and the Wright Brothers. I remarked to Bob "why can't we go to Kitty Hawk and shoot there". We both agreed and that is how the "opening shot" was completed.

You must realize that when you are "on location" you have to use any "local points of interest" to make the best picture. Brain storming is a good way to get the ideas flowing for the team. The Kitty Hawk location was not local; it was about 2 hours by air and all day by car. Because there are few who visit the monument due to its remote location that made it a unique value.

Bob found Don Brockman, a local TV stand up personality in Greensboro, NC that had the time to do our movie.

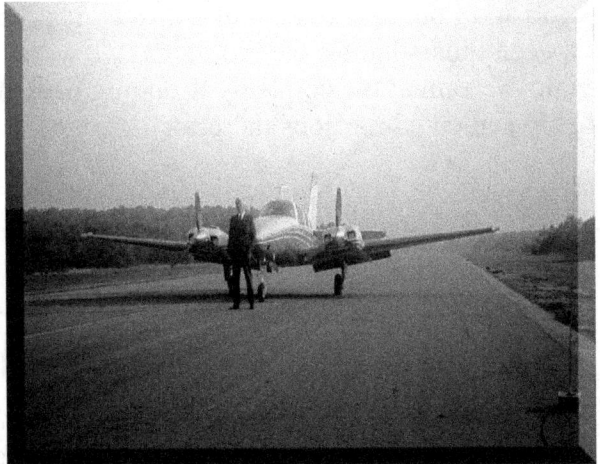

The shot: During a minute and a half of "on camera dialog",
Brockman was standing on the runway at Kitty Hawk with the Baron landing behind him.

The Camera work at Kitty Hawk:

The camera work was extremely good because the "Depth of Field" at full zoom showed an aircraft landing on the strip "out of focus" at first, but people who knew airplanes realized immediately what was going on. Then it came into focus with the props still turning until it was in perfect focus just 12 inches away from Mr. Brockman's back.

When Brockman delivered the scripted tag line: *"**We think the Wright Brothers would have been Pleased**"* while glancing over his shoulder at the plane with sound effects of a bird chirping and with the crackle of the hot engines as they cool, the scene was electric. The audience at the Sales Show went crazy with loud and long standing applause. They had never seen anything this outstanding in a film from Beech, Beech was ultra conservative.

Bob and I breathed a long and heave breath and shook each others hands, we did it, and we were the official AV team at the company. Looking back we probably cemented our jobs there for 10 years.

Production Notes At Kitty Hawk

Dave Palay, the pilot, would radio us when he reached a certain landmark about 1 min 45sec out was our "cue" to roll camera and sound and have Brockman start his dialog. We had worked out the time from that landmark to completing his landing that would have him stop just short of Brockman's back at the end of the dialog.

I was doing 16mm Sync Sound and used a Vega wireless mike for the opening shot. I am standing off to the side as far as my sync cord would go because it was safer incase there was any messy accident. However, Bob was stuck out in the middle of the runway behind the "16mm Arri BL" camera. Audio of all takes had to be the same quality sound to cut well, so after we started there was no adjusting of anything.

In retrospect this was an extremely dangerous shot and Don Brockman did not know the dangers involved in what he was doing and we did not tell him. Working on a runway or near a runway is best left to professionals, after saying that; we did it all the time for the "great shots" of aircraft landing or taking off over our heads.

Our safety system consisted of a two-way radio with the pilot. If something went wrong it could have been messy and the nearest medical office was miles away with a car which we did not have.

What proved to be a great cut was a shot of Brockman from the "side" during the shot with the "First Flight Monument" visible in the trees.

A mistake of leaving a camera cable out of the camera box at Greensboro was discovered during the setup at Kitty Hawk. This required a 4 hour flight from Kitty Hawk back to pickup the cable. When everything was ready Bob almost called the shoot off because of the weather.

On the Barrier Islands of North Carolina the rain would roll in, the humidity would go up almost daily making work out on the runway close to unbearable. When temperature, humidity or wind would change it would affect the landing distance of the aircraft and our calculations for safety.

Location 3: Atlantic Ocean

Viewing the pictures taken off shore in the Atlantic, from Myrtle Beach, it looked very easy and it was. The shot was of the girls waving at the plane as it went by only lasted 10 seconds in the finished film.

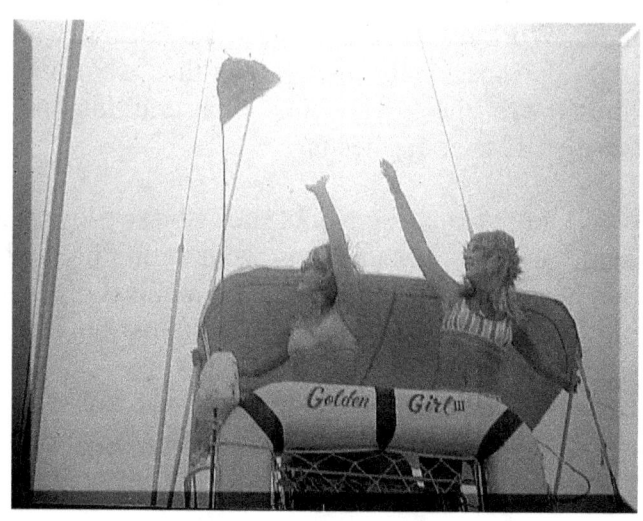

It turned out to be a half day outing with some "scared and sea sick girls". Is seems that we forgot to ask them if they could handle the waves on the boat. While flying in small aircraft Bob and I had become use to the "bumps and sways" so we were not affected.

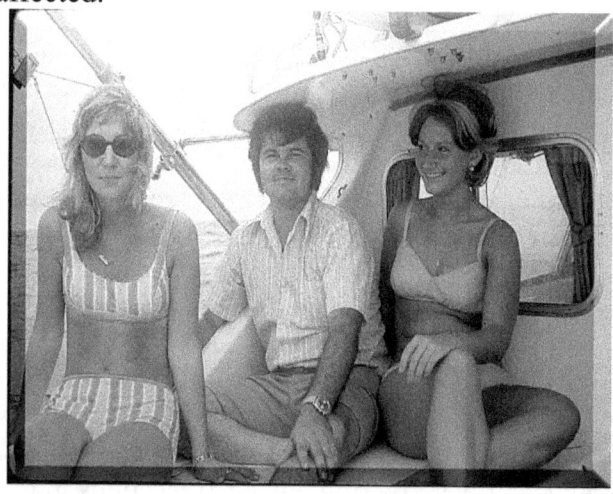

Note: Being on a photo crew you enjoy each moment when you can.

The Atlantic boat location was somewhat of a free day for me.

Just some "wild sound" and no lip sync sound.

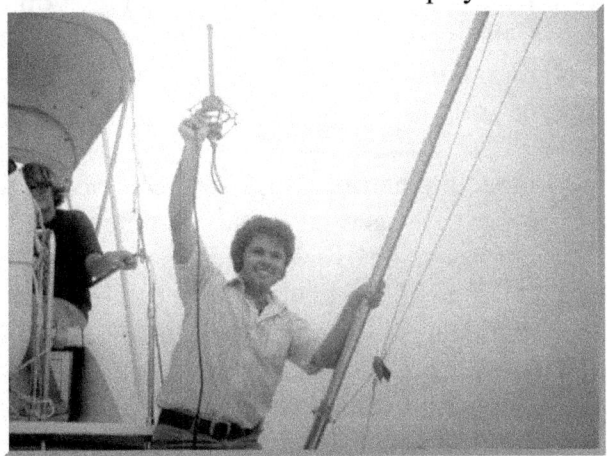

I am holding the Academy Award winning ElectroVoice 642 Shotgun mike for wild sound. Notice the "looped cable" and shock mount; to reduce sound pops out of mike.

Location 4: Beech Mountain, NC

The shots at Beech Mountain were used only because the "on camera" interview of a customer playing golf with the pilot. He explained how using his Baron he was able to get away from his office in Charlotte and fly to Beech Mountain for a golf vacation at his "chalet" and then could return in very short time due to the Baron. There was one other point; Beech Mountain was spelled the same way as "Beech" Aircraft, our company, and we even shot "Dorothy and Toto" at the mountain's theme park.

Production Notes at Beech Mountain

I used the Vega Wireless mike while the customers were out putting around on the golf course; this was way out of range for the EV 642 Shotgun mike and I had to be tethered to the camera for sync sound.

I taped the narration part of the owner on the golf course. It was used for story content and to cut to time, for visuals over the picture was of the Baron taking off and landing at Beech Mountain. Back in the day, we were treated like VIP's. We landed at Beech Mountain, they took us to a chalet on the mountain where we spent two nights and then went to the theme park. All of this service for this "film crew" from out west and we repaid them by putting the theme park in the movie.

Movie Acceptance at the Annual Sales Show:

Premier of the Baron movie: At the annual Sales Show that fall, the audience gasped and applauded when the Baron came up behind Brockman.

This project cemented our jobs for years. Movies up until then were tired "nuts and bolts" style industrial flicks with a heavy dose of specifications and little creativity.

Since this film was more entertainment versus the hard sell, the audience acceptance was more wide spread. This was a big gamble because it was so different but sometimes you have to think outside the box and this time it worked.

The down side was the background scenes for the "Credits"; where Bob shot memorabilia of "The Red Baron of WWI".

In the final cut many found that the credit shots seemed to go on forever. Another big gamble, "Credits" for an Industrial movie. The credits also burned our names, for good or bad, into our management's brains so it had to be better than what they had seen before.

As with any film some parts of the production were out of our control; the time it took to send a finished work print to the lab with instructions on assembly required days of work. One of the people that were featured on camera in the film was the owner of the FBO at Greensboro NC. When we got the film back from the lab the name burn in for his on camera part was spelled wrong.

We did not have time to correct the spelling and get the film back from the lab. Since he was in the audience we had no choice but to close the gate on the moving film during the show blacking out the screen. It was only 3 seconds but it seemed as though it was 3 minutes.

Today correcting such a problem takes only a few minutes to run another copy on the editor.

A Story of Cowboys and Airplanes

The "New Pioneer" – Actor Rex Allen

Award Winner of "Creative Excellence" by the Industrial Film Festival

Film Location – on a ranch just north of Jackson Hole, Wyoming

This location is near a stream very close to the headwaters of the Snake River from the Yellowstone Plateau.

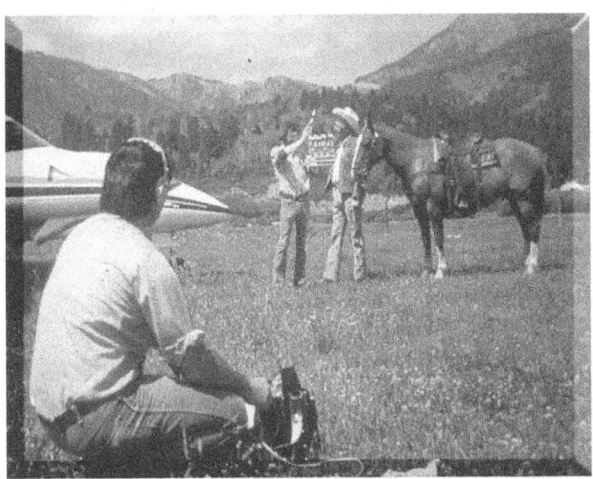

Me and my Nagra

The Opening Scene "The Old West": On the ground a Cowboy (Rex Allen) walking his horse (looking at the camera) talking about what happened to horse rustlers in the old west.

He comes to a stop next to a "very hot airplane" parked in a field. Rex would transition his on camera intro to the next scene in the pilot's seat flying over Montana. The narration track of Rex was running with background music or effects of engine noise.

The day we shot the opening scene I injured my back carrying the Nagra III around and spent most of the next day on my back in pain at the motel in Jackson Hole. I could not do the Air shots with Rex setting in the pilot's seat of the Duke, but Doug shot the scene flawlessly while "Doctor Bob" gave me some pills and stayed with me.

On this trip I learned what a "Sciatic Nerve" is and how it can stop you in your tracks. I was able to work the next day. Be careful lifting and turning photo equipment, the Nagra weighed in at about 20 lbs.

The "New Cowboy" from Costa Mesa

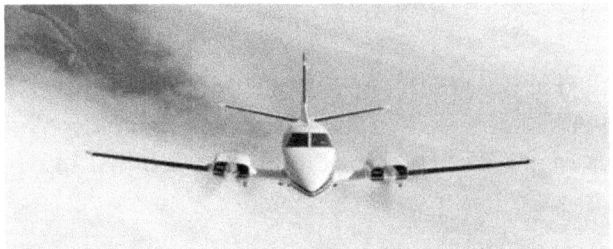

After Rex's scene in the cockpit, we cut to air to air and transition to modern day business type "owner" flying from Costa Mesa, CA to Dallas, TX with the appropriate air shots as Rex continues his narration. One extra nice thing about the photo subject plane; it looks like it is going 300 MPH just setting on the ramp.

The Quite Little West Texas Town of Lubbock

One of the contrasts marketing wanted to explore with this film was the extended range of the "new Duke", so they showed a refueling shot in a "West Texas" town as a "time waster" for the business man. Rex wanted to tone down the script and down play the fueling stop as such a negative.

Much later I found the reason for the script change was that he was born on a ranch in Mud Springs Canyon a short distance from Willcox, Arizona that's just a few days ride to "West Texas".

In Dallas the shooting took place at the restaurant and club of the Sheridan Hotel on Mockingbird near Love Field. This hotel has change to Park Inn Hotel Dallas Love Field if you are looking.

minutes to forget you were talking with a movie star.

He did stand out with his big white hat he wore everywhere. Rex's son carried on his dad's voice over career with a voice that sounded just like his dad's.

This was the first time I had the opportunity to work with and get to know a professional movie star. I learned that even though some one has been in many films, he could be a regular guy. Bob had the knowledge of how to shoot a film to cover mistakes and deficiencies of the talent.

Note: "Take 23"? It is not cool to keep going over and over each line, it is much better to break up shots into small chunks with change of angle cutaways to cover flubs.

We found out during an evening shot that the mosquitoes at Jackson are the size of small birds and they do attack in swarms.

The crew for the New Pioneer was Bob Braddy Director, Doug Ambler 2nd camera, me for sound, Kenny Freeman production assistant, two marketing pilots; Steve Millham and Steve Sayre.

We actually used this hotel a few times as it was close for I-35 traffic and also close to Love field where we later shot a King Air movie.

We were happy to mention hotels like the Sheridan in Dallas as they provided us with extra rooms and even room service for casting calls when required.

My Time with the Cowboys

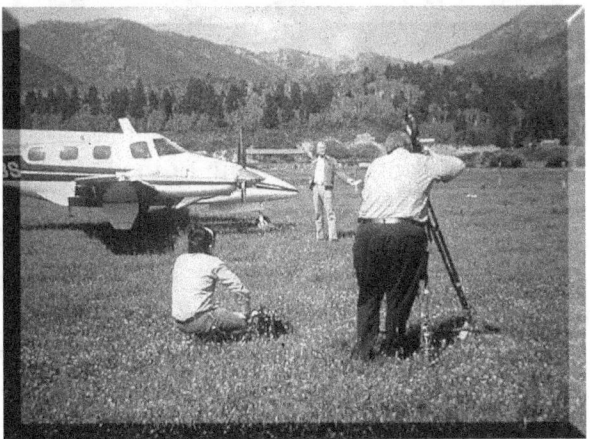
Camera, Sound, Action

Rex Allen was down to earth and a very nice guy, unexpected for movie talent. He was a "laidback" cowboy. After shooting in Jackson Hole, he invited the film crew to his good friend Slim Pickens's (Major "King" Kong in Doctor Strangelove) cabin on Bear Creek for some trout fishing.

After shooting hours, we sat around the lobby / bar at the hotel and would tell stories about other movies he was in, all the time drinking his favorite drink, a Bourbon and Branch Water. It took about 2

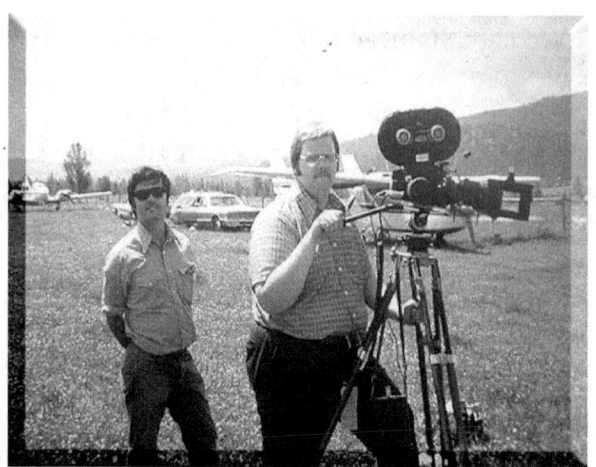

A candid shot of Bob Braddy with his Arri BL
and I during the shooting of the Duke.

This is my "Jack Nicholson look" before I even
knew who he was. Notice the "Crew car" (station
wagon) in background with doors open, probably
holding one of the crew or Rex taking a quick nap.
Bob looks very serous for some reason while I was
having a blast.

I am sure that he wants to finish and get the
crew and cast out of the heat and back to the hotel
for an afternoon drink. Even though Jackson Hole,
Wyoming is a very nice place in the spring time, but
with its high altitude you can get a sun burn rather
quickly.

Still shots were used in the marketing material
and shot by a very young Paul Bowen and his
assistant. I ran across Paul a few more times doing
shoots for the T1A, Beechjet and the T6A JPATS
Trainer.

Paul Bowen was with me doing the Chapter on Extreme Environmental Conditions shoot. He was doing the stills and I was shooting video in the back with the doors of the Baron off.

The New Pioneer, The Rematch

Even after completing the shoot we got back to the factory and found that they changed the model name of the airplane to the "B 60". Because of the narration track that we did at a local radio station in Jackson Whole with Rex, it no longer worked!

I was dispatched to Salt Lake City where Rex was working on another project. One afternoon I cornered him in a motel room for about 2 hours just long enough to cut a new narration tract and get back on the airplane going to Wichita. Then it was back to transfer all tracks to 16mm magnetic tape for final editing.

Production Notes "The New Pioneer" A Story of Cowboys and Airplanes

Bob was shooting with an Arri 16BL (Blimp Housing) with "Neopilot" sync using Kodak 7252 and a 85 filter. (Later we went to "Crystal Sync" **no** cables but still needed a Clapboard) Pilot Sync was developed by Hollywood to keep the sound and pictures synchronized during shooting because with out sync the sound or picture would start to "drift" and you could not lock or lip sync for an extended time, and it would become a disaster the longer the shot.

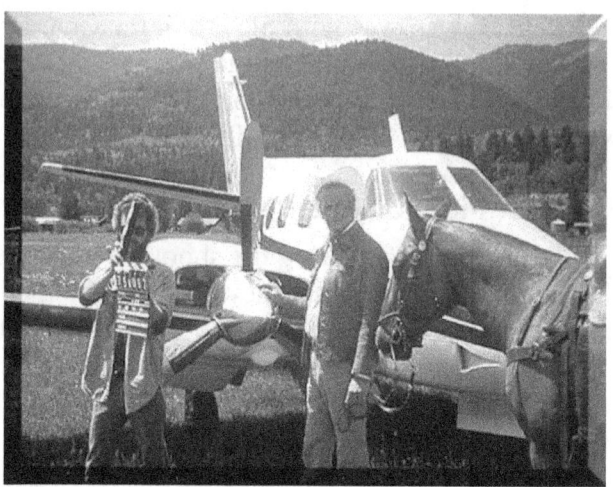

Kenny, Rex and Big Red

    I was using a new **Professional Vega II** wireless mike to hear and record sound on a **Nagra III** reel to reel recorder, the shot was a Wide shot (WS). Kenny Freeman is shown holding the Clapboard in front of Rex Allen; we had to keep track of the scenes.

    The Clapboard, needed for double system sound, "marked" a sync point that was used in the editing. The camera shot of the clapboard and the sound of the clap with the scene identifying made it ease to find and cut the work print and the magnetic 16mm film strip together so that the sound and picture were synced.

    Using a synchronizer, you could keep each part locked together. Some times you would have more than two audios and two pictures locked and then you could cut between.

    Rex "borrowed" a horse from the ranch where we shot at in Jackson Whole. This is a MS

(Medium Shot) for a line or two of on camera dialog. This type of cut (to change camera angles) is used for editing where the action in the shot is wrong or the talent muffs his lines.

Before the "Predator" there was the "Streaker"

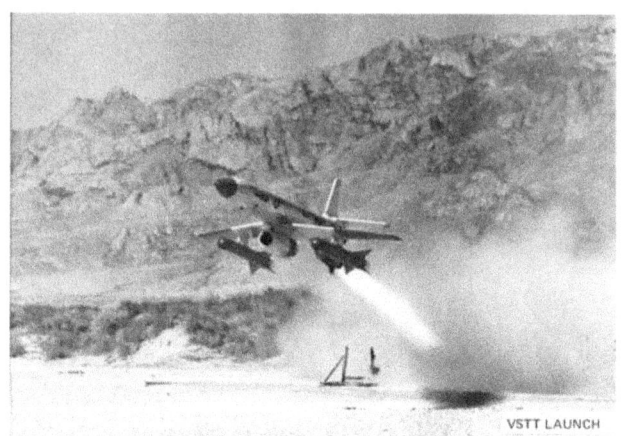

VSTT LAUNCH

MQM107A Streaker

The military designated two of our target missiles, the AQM37 and the MQM107, each with a specific use and mission its own code name.

The recoverable MQM107A called the "Streaker" was a VSTT or Variable Speed Training Target. The missile was developed in 1972 to the requirements of the United States Army Aviation and Missile Commands. The subsonic missile can be launched by the use of a rocket booster accelerating it until the jet engine takes over.

Usually it will tow a target that will be used for gunnery practice or IR missile firings.

Doug Ambler: "Getting the right camera angle usually involved thinking on the fly. Our trip to Alamogordo, New Mexico, on the White Sands

Missile Range, involved a documentary highlighting the VSST (Variable speed training target). The VSST was basically a jet-powered missile with wings.

The VSST was designed to be launched from a stand. The onboard jet was only for keeping the VSST flying once it was accelerated to flying speed by an expendable JATO solid rocket motor."

We were to document the storage, preparation for the flight, the launch, the control and the recovery after the end of mission chute deployment.

Every thing except the launch was pretty much a standard documentation. The launch was the most exciting and the hardest to capture due to safety constraints.

Later, I would spend a week to document the preparation and the launch of the MQM on the other side of the United States at Tyndall Air Force Base in Florida where they have annual gunnery competition.

The cool thing about the MQM107 was that after launch the target was controlled by ground personnel watching a plotter to determine where the target was and where to send the target next. Our movie described building, testing and the use for training.

It also had a section about the future uses as a UAV to find and detect targets on the battle field. We did not understand that UAVs would change the way war is waged then, but now with the use of UAV's in Afghanistan and other areas, it was eerie that we demonstrated what a UAV could do 20 years before it happened.

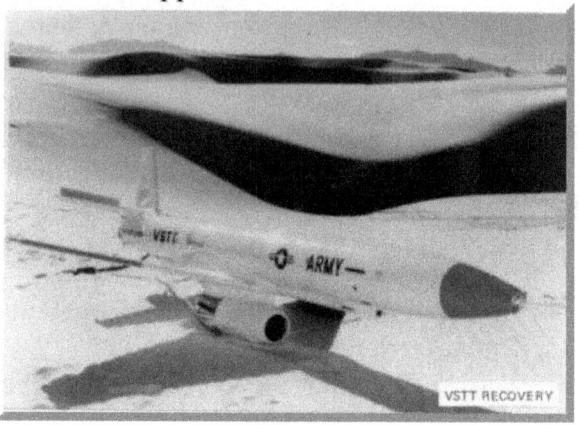

Production Notes "MQM107A" – "The Streaker"

The MQM107A film was requested by the Contract Sales department to demonstrate the utility of the missile for export and domestic use. Ground launched on a stand with a JATO rocket, then controlled with a ground station it was a very reliable system and could have it's mission changed in flight.

Shooting crew of 3; Bob Braddy, Doug Ambler and I, were to spend a week at El Paso Texas with a drive of about an hour each day to White Sands NM for shots at the prep area, the recovery area and launch stands.

Since we were out in the middle of nowhere, lunch each day became a problem. We just "missed" lunch on most days rather than driving an hour to Alamogordo New Mexico.

This film was shot just after the "New Pioneer Duke" movie, and we started at the construction site just north of Bolder Colorado at our Beech Bolder Plant where they also built Cryogenics tanks for the space program.

Special shots of the launch of the missile, the most impressive stage of the flight, required everyone to be behind or inside of the launch bunker. This was a safety requirement before the launch and as it turned out a very smart requirement.

Doug wanted to get a ground level shot looking back as it launched over the camera and a shot directly overhead as well. To trigger the cameras he had to buy some string and tape it to the switch in the battery belt.

Due to the danger from the rocket motor we were required to hide behind the bunker. This required about 100+ feet of string. I knew that the JATO motor was powerful so he tied the camera to a medium sized rock to hold it in place.

The camera on the ground was set to 100 FPS (frames per second) to show the launch in slow motion. During the countdown, Doug held off as long as he could to account for only 15 seconds of film.

Unfortunately the countdown was also to allow for the electrical umbilical to detach from the missile prior to the launch. The overhead camera looked great but the forward camera only showed the umbilical dropping.

After the spectacular launch, Doug walked out to retrieve the forward camera. It was nowhere in sight. After some searching he located it several hundred feet back still tied to the rock. The lens was unscathed! After that, he had a healthy respect for the force behind a rocket motor.

Note: During a later launch, one where we needed only 24 FPS (Sound Speed), I modified the receiver from my Vega wireless mike system to close a relay when a carrier from the mike's transmitter was received. This allowed a more positive remote controlled switch to power the camera from the battery located next to the camera and can operate both off & on remotely.

A video of the MQM is here.

AQM37C "Jayhawks" Never flew this Fast

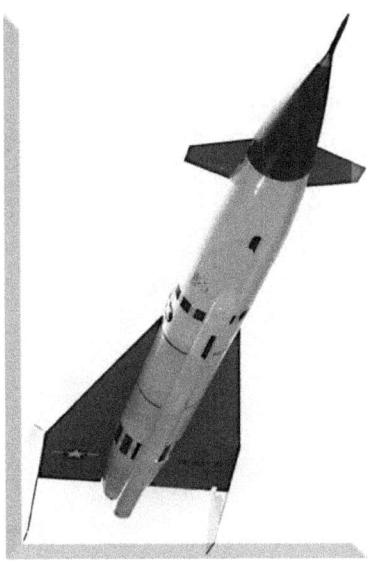

The AQM37 super sonic target was called the "Jayhawk" used by the Navy for target practice mostly over the Pacific at Point Mugu, California to simulate missile threats to ships and aircraft.

The expendable AQM37 can go as low as 50 feet or do mach 4.7 at 112,000 feet.

This missile is **Pre-Programmed before launch** with altitude and speed settings and using storable fuels. Some variants were the "Sea skimmer", the "Sandpiper" and the "HAST" usually air launched by a Phantom F4 diving to near supersonic speed to get a good boost phase before launch.

I shot some of the preparation for launch and the Navy would supply me with air to air shots.

The rare occasion of the AQM-37CEP extended performance target was launched from an

F-4 aircraft at 50,000 ft altitude traveling at MACH 1.5.

Eight of these targets were specially modified for flight safety purposes to be flown at WSMR as targets for the Standard Missile program SM-2 Block IV in 1993.

The targets were supported by crews from the Pacific Missile Range at Point Mugu, CA. Launch of the target from the F-4 aircraft occurred virtually over the Albuquerque International Airport requiring special road blocks south of Albuquerque, use of the north range extension co-use area and evacuation of most of WSMR up-range areas. (From WSMR history.org)

How to Catch the Bad Guys, Use a

Maritime Patrol Aircraft

If you have ever watched spy shows on TV you may have seen some of the "Interdiction" aircraft videos. Inferred video is so good now at catching the bad guys I don't know why they try to get away.

The most notable Maritime Patrol Aircraft was the Navy's EP-3 Orion. The Orion made news when one was forced to land in Hainan China in 2001. The Chinese held the crew of 23 for a few days. We have been making "Special Mission" aircraft for years and now the technology is very good. Inferred can see people or changes in heat temperature in total darkness. They can see cargo ships and tell if they are carrying cargo in their holds. SAR or Search and Rescue versions using IR are much more successful than just looking out the window.

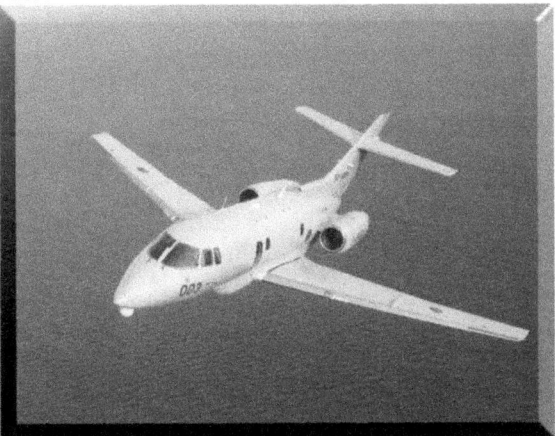

Hawker U125 Japanese Maritime Patrol

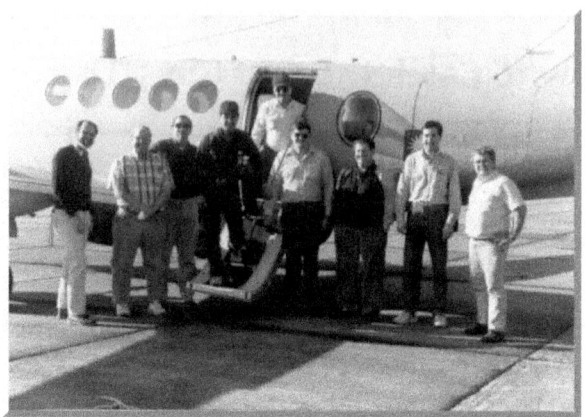

Photo Mission Crew: On left; John Cook Still Photographer, two Special Mission Experimental salesmen with two Experimental mechanics and two Flight Test pilots for the Special Mission aircraft. The photo aircraft Flight Test pilot Dennis Hildreth next to me on the far right.

The aircraft was a "Special Mission" Maritime Patrol King Air, with a huge radar dome on its belly seen behind John. Tip tanks out of picture and special observation windows aft of the door on both sides.

Special Mission aircraft usually have at least one or sometimes as high as three tightly packed radar operator consoles in the cabin.

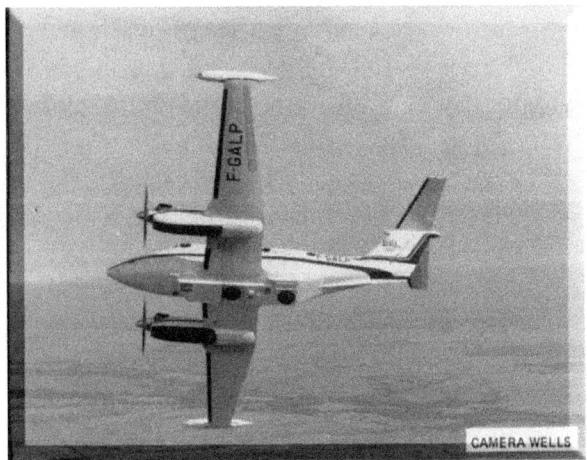

The Special Mission 200 is a very good platform as it could fly on patrol for an extended time with the "Tip Tank" fuel option and with much less vibration than a helicopter.

This Photo Mission was one of the more difficult ones due to the "photo plane" configuration requirement. This mission required both Stills and Video be shot on this "export" version special mission aircraft.

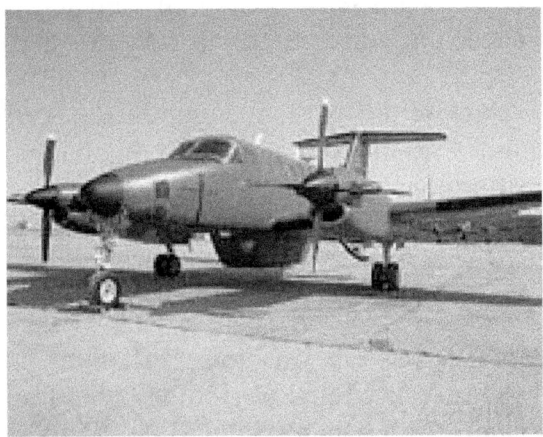

The mission was based in Port Arthur TX, BB-343 had an "Experimental ticket", and so the cabin door could be removed before the shoot to get low altitude still pictures of the Maritime Aircraft.

The shoot involved flying the two King Airs in close formation over the Gulf of Mexico about 100 miles out, looking for oil platforms and shrimp boats to film as background. The mission was to get photos of the aircraft to show its Maritime Patrol Missions, which included these ships and oil derricks being patrolled.

One picture is worth a thousand words can not be over stated.

To complete the shoot, photos out of the cabin door required the left engine to be shutdown because the exhaust blurred stills.

Cabin noise made getting shots for John's still photo's very difficult to set up because of communication between us was next to impossible because of the noise, so he and I used hand signals even inside the cabin of the camera ship

So picture the two twin engine King Airs in formation with the lead aircraft having only one engine turning and a big whole in the left side fuselage flying low and slow. All this takes place about 100 miles off of shore over the Gulf of Mexico at about 500 feet above sea level.

Note: John Cook was doing still photography out the side door while I was doing video from the belly camera. John was using a **Hasselblad** 2 ¼ by 2 ¼, (120x120) and I would radio instructions "closer out forward or back" to adjust the subject plane for his shot. Still shots were usually at the wrong distance for my system. John would also give hand signals out the door to the other aircraft.

Before this mission John and I discussed how to control the shots and he thought a throat mike would be best but I was unable to find the WWII type microphone in surplus stores. It was like herding cats, at least a dozen huge variables to control going at 200 MPH.

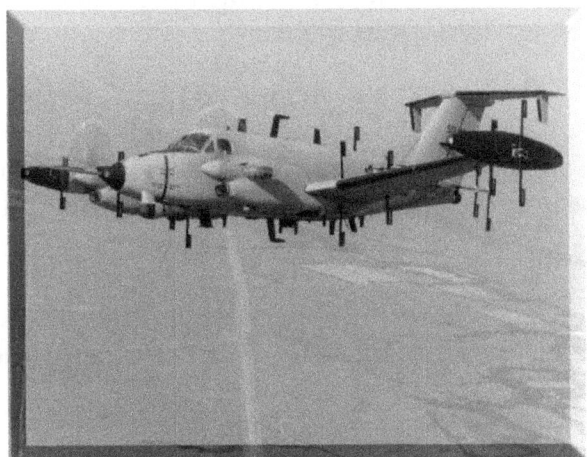

RC12N Special Mission Intel Aircraft actually fly's. "If you have enough power a brick can fly"

Correcting Color Problems

If you have ever flown low over the Gulf of Mexico within 100 miles of the shore between New Orleans and Galveston you will notice one problem; the water can be very brown.

To make this water blue you have to get a low altitude shot late in the day, an hour before sunset with the sun to your back. This late day sun angle would allow the water to pickup the blue from the sky and help the pictures.

Whoever set this schedule did not provide for flexible shooting so I could not get the water blue because we shot during the worst time of the day, 10AM till 3PM.

When I shot the same type of shots after 4:00PM over the Pacific near Santa Cruz Island in 1999 the water was blue. In retrospect since the mission was already set for the Mississippi Delta, blue was just not available.

My Coordinator Job was to find a suitable background and then stage all aircraft in formation, to approach, keeping the sun in correct angle and the airplanes flying in the correct direction and speed.

As you can imagine, the setup to get all the shots with all parameters perfect is an extreme drain on the crews of both aircrafts.

I was facing aft toward the tail and looking at a color TV while talking on the communications radio to the other pilots to get them in position, all with tremendous wind whipping around in the cabin due to the door being off.

The cabin wind vibration made setting shots for John's still camera very difficult even with the left engine shut down. Just putting the camera in the jet stream would instantly induce camera shake.

. Quite often we would have a still photographer on board too, on many occasions he would shoot through a side window with the "polarizing lens of the window removed. On some occasions we would fly with both the escape hatch removed and the door removed on the opposite side of the fuselage removed and that proved to be very interesting as far as noise and wind turbulence goes...

Can It Fly with Ice? The MU2

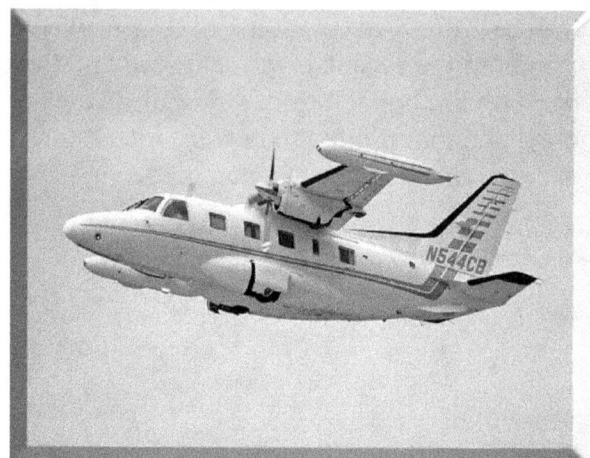

The Subject Aircraft: Mitsubishi MU-2 corporate prototype.

MU2 Crew: Pilot, hired by Mitsubishi, Corporate Pilot and video systems photographer Mike Barnes with 8 cameras.

The Photo Ship: BB-343 camera ship and its ability to shoot video tests

The Mission: Find and photograph Ice build up and Ice removal on wings of MU-2

After a few high profile accidents with the Mitsubishi MU2, and a **CBS 60 Minutes exposé** with associated litigation cases, it was necessary to document how the aircraft flew with a large ice load.

To put the accusations to rest, Mitsubishi contracted with a company in Dublin, Ohio to provide proof that the aircraft would fly correctly if managed like the manual required. The MU2 was fast and any fast airplane requires the pilot to think ahead of the airplane or as some people say, "stay ahead of the power curve".

The photo ship; a King Air BB-343, would fly below the icing level in clear air while the MU2 would fly above in the icing area to pickup one or two inches on the wings.

After accumulation of ice for the test the MU2 would descend to rendezvous with us and we would document the ice load. Then the MU2 would use it's de-ice system and shed the ice. We would video the accumulation and the resulting ice shedding.

I spent a full week flying 10 hours a day, from San Francisco to L.A. to Dallas in near icing conditions near cloud layers.

The BB-343 Crew was two pilots a still photographer and me shooting video. I did get a little tired of being bounced around all day, but my pilot would break the boredom once in a while by rolling the King Air.

Production Notes for the MU2 Icing Tests

Note: We would get weather reports of where the cloud icing was happening. Then we would file a flight plan to take us to that area. Most assuredly the weather people thought we were crazy and maybe we were, trying to find clouds with icing conditions.

Most pilots would stay away from these conditions since icing is one of the leading causes of aircraft accidents. Bouncing around in icing and clouds all day for days on end is not a pleasant way to spend time, but that is what we did.

PTZ Mount camera location on the BB343 was just aft of the lower rotating beacon. On the BB343, being an Experimental KA200 that was used to prototype the KA300; the beacon was located farther forward and almost in line with the leading edge of the wing.

The PTZ camera could get some of the best shots from 90 degrees left around to 90 degrees right. At times I could swing the camera to straight ahead, when working with the pilot, to 90 degrees high to straight down.

The faring was designed to "pre wrap" the camera cable one full revolution so that as the Pan Tilt, when it rotated its 355 degrees, it would un-wrap the camera cable into the hollow faring during its rotation.

The camera, when facing aft, would be half unwrapped, so not only the operator needed to know all the shooting parameters, but what the condition of the camera, wind and which way he could direct the plane to have a shooting motion without running into the pan tilt "stops".

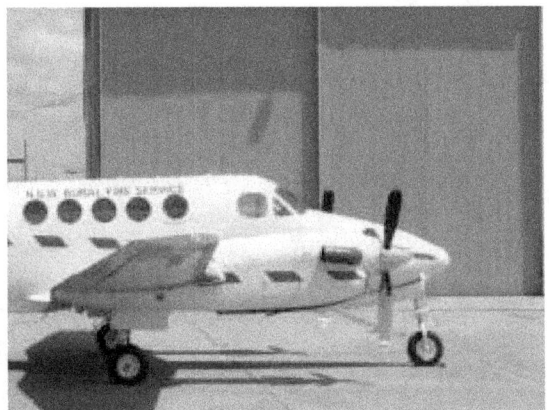

King Air Escape Hatch Location: forward
window in cabin

Escape Hatch: The Beech King Air 200,
shown above, as with all King Airs have an Escape
Hatch with a window located on the right side in the
forward cabin. The escape hatch can be seen
outlined just below the word "...Service".

This hatch can be removed prior to flight on
"Experimental Aircraft" like the BB343, to provide
a very windy and cold opening to shoot out of for
air to air photography.

Camera Pedestal: I had to design a removable
camera pedestal to fit to the chair seat tracks on
both a King Air and a 1900 airliner that would
swing into the window opening for a solid shot. We
usually had a three man crew, the Pilot, the Escape
Hatch shooter and me shooting with the Belly
Camera.

Extreme Environmental Flying

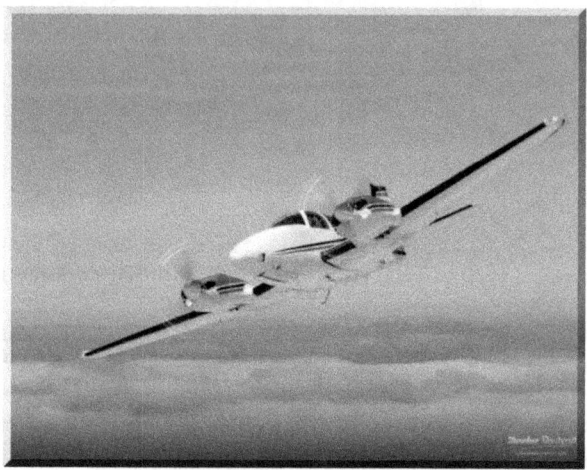

Model 58 Photo Plane

On one photo shoot I was to be teamed with the Paul Bowen in San Diego only in December, but when we got to Flagstaff Arizona and checked the weather the storm over San Diego did not move out of the area as expected. It was decided to switch the primary shooting spot to Seattle and allow the weather to move out of San Diego.

Change of Plans

The flight from Flagstaff to Seattle was beautiful flying at 3,000 or 4,000 AGL, feet above ground level over Utah, the Great Salt Lake and Mount Saint Helens was great. I did have a problem; my flying gear was not rated for the expected cold of this new environment which required me to get a cold suite when we got to Seattle. Stopping in a ski shop I found what I thought I needed and the clerk said it was rated at minus10 degrees. I found that it needed to be rated at -20 and 200 MPH for the shoot. With my cold suite over my winter coat we started by departing Seattle in the morning, and then heading for and circling above the peak of Mount Rainer Washington (14,410 FT) near Seattle with the doors off in the Baron, which turned out to be a memorable flight. I was in the back of the baron airplane for over 2 hours in -20 degree outside temperature and 200 MPH wind stream circling in the cabin and blowing directly on me. The wind-chill was off the charts. Flying at 15,000ft, is over 3000ft above the safe oxygen level. However the pain of shooting was outweighed by the very crisp clean air at altitude, coupled with the great background, the snow capped peak of Mount Rainer, along with the subject plane a red and white Beechjet 400A made for some beautiful pictures.

Extreme Pain

I had a case of painful frost bite and took 4 hours to regain blood flow to face and hands by getting up close and personal with a pot bellied stove when we refueled at Astoria Oregon. I flew the next leg of the shoot to San Diego in the warm cabin of the subject plane, a Beechjet 400A. During that flight from Astoria to San Diego they used the background of the rocky Oregon cost, very nice, but the sun being about noon was not in the best angle for great pictures. This became shots of convince but not super quality. They did have it easy; the trip south got warmer the further they went and it was at a warm 1,500 AGL.

New Shooting Technique

Shooting in San Diego was much warmer. We used a B25 that never got over 3,000ft at 200MPH, and outside air temperature thankfully at 70 degrees, only when the sun went down did it get cold. Paul Bowen would shoot stills from the tail of the old WWII bomber.

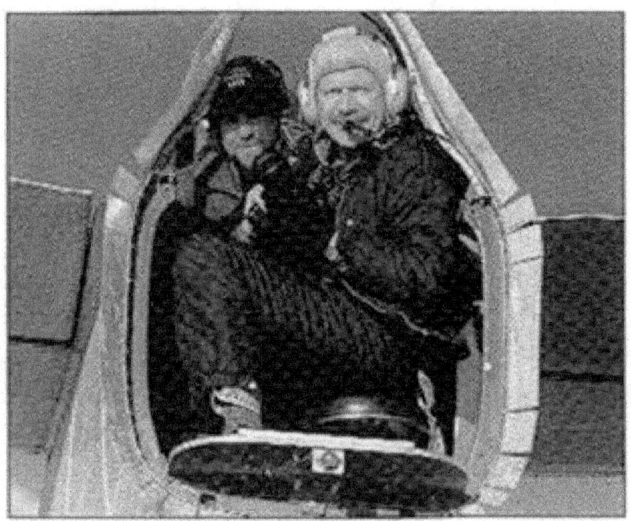

Paul in the tail of a B25

Often the company would hire Paul and a B25 for stills to get angles that we couldn't get with our company cameral ship. Contract photography was a hard pill for **our company** still photographers to swallow; it said our photographers were not good enough. Looking back, our photogs were good enough, but they could not develop the connections to rent a B25 or a Learjet in California when they were working from Wichita, because we did not have the opportunities to make the connections they got someone who could talk to the right people and Paul was hired to "Make it happen". Paul Bowen was the premier air to air photographer and had the connections and was available at that time, and one of the easiest guys to work with you'll find.

I would shoot whatever I could from the "waist gunner" position. Shooting was from about 5PM to around 8PM what is known as the "magic hour".

As the sun goes down the background of the city, in this case San Diego starts to go dark with street lights while the aircraft's color temp warms from daylight 5600K blue approaching close to Tungsten color, 3200K, then Paul would fire off a strobe to "pop" the airplane from its background while holding some of the warm sunset light.

The trick is to have the background in this case San Diego in shadow because on the ground the sun had set while at 3,000 feet the aircraft was still in the last few minutes before sunset. This condition only lasts for a few minuets so you have to be in position and ready at that time or you will miss it.

Note: This technique is great for stills, but for video I would have to have a strobe that fires 30 times a second, which would blind the pilots in the subject aircraft.

Money Shot in Trail

Some of Paul's shots from the B25 are thrilling when you think of how he did it; picture a full frame shot (close up) head on of an airplane pulling up at 80 to 90 degrees' with the back drop of an airport below.

I was not there but they must have been in formation doing flat out 230 MPH, then over the airport both aircraft with the subject aircraft in "Trail" formation, did a maximum clime and then Paul only had a few seconds to snap the shots before the King Air or Jet would over take the B25 and have to break off the formation before collision. Inside it would have been a ride not unlike a roller-coaster and Paul hanging there in the tail with just a few feet of air between him and the other aircraft.

I have pictures and videos of our shoots with more details at http://acfs.biz

A Run-In with the US Government!

"The Tradition of Excellence"

In 1989 we started filming the a 1900C film in Telluride, Colorado at the airport which has a very long and wide cement runway with a very deep dip in the middle so you could see the airplane seem to "appear" and takeoff. That take off shot is in the finished film.

Telluride, a ski town, is almost deserted during the spring and summer, when we were there to film, so we could do about anything that was legal. We parked the airplane on the north end "turn-around" and got out for a picture. I believe that there was only one flight, a 1900C/D that comes from Denver the entire day in the off season. We had shot some footage at the old Denver Stapleton airport, of ground activities located at the end Concourse B where the commuter airlines come in. This footage would intercut with what we were going to get on this south west trip.

We knew that we wanted to shoot at Mesa Airlines at Mesa, AZ, Navajo Reservoir, NM and Lake Powell, AZ, because Mesa used the 1900C type of airplane and I have shot at Lake Powell, which has great blue waters and mountains close to Page AZ.

From Page AZ it is just a few (Air) minutes to lots of scenic landscapes in the Utah, Arizona and New Mexico region.

As it normally goes, we would do locations of convenience or spots the locals suggest might be interesting visually. Many times we get the best shots and most interesting stories using spur of the moment filming locations.

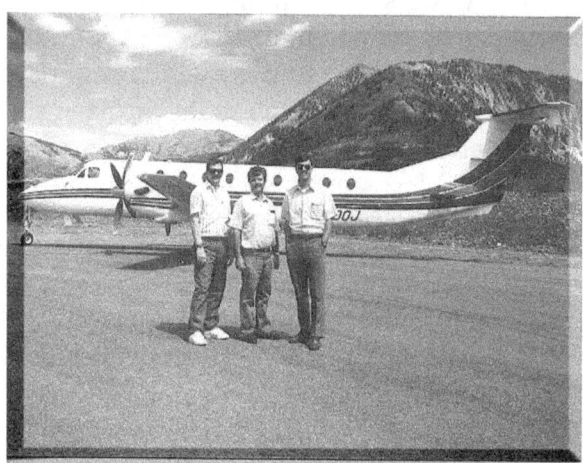

Crew: Mike Barnes, Richard Young, and Tony Marlow Pilot at Telluride CO.

My good friend Mike Barnes, Video Photographer, me and Tony Marlow our trusted Test Pilot would fly all over the south west getting shots and interviews of 1900 users.

The airplane was N1900J, the prototype 1900C, a highly modified twin turboprop with no interior and just 4 chairs in an empty 19 passenger fuselage.

Without a lot of interior weight and baggage the airplane handled like a big sports car which would prove essential later.

After the stop at Telluride we went on to Mesa, Arizona where we interview the operations chief for

Mesa Airlines and then at Ship Rock, Arizona where we had shot excellent "air to air" of another 1900C and then on to Navaho Lake the next day for some great pre-dawn takeoff shots.

How to get Pre Dawn Photos

To get the dawn takeoff shots we left our motel about 4:00AM, we sometimes checked out the night before if no one was going to be on duty at 4:00AM. We went to the airport at Mesa, loaded gear with flashlights, took off and flew about 30 minutes to an unmanned strip on top of a mesa at Navajo Lake NM all before twilight.

It is essential that whenever we shoot outside we put the filter to daylight with .3 ND and never press the white balance of the camera, this gives the appropriate warmth to the picture that is perfect to capture the golden hour.

As a rule, I only white balance a camera to match unusual camera conditions such as when shooting people in a hanger that has mercury-vapor lamps. The eye is tricked very quickly into seeing what it thinks is white while the camera will not fall for the off color and show it as not white.

We landed at an airport with out lights at night on top of this mesa. We unloaded the gear and setup the cameras at the east end in the dark. Then we had the pilot do some takeoff and landings as the sun came up and continued after sunrise. So by 9:00AM we had already put in a 5 hour day.

After we were satisfied with the dawn shot we loaded back up and returned the 30 min for the interview with Ken Widger, the operations manager at Mesa Airlines, another 5 hours. Next stop flying around "Ship Rock NM for 2 hours, the Navajo's call it "Winged Rock", with two 1900C aircraft.

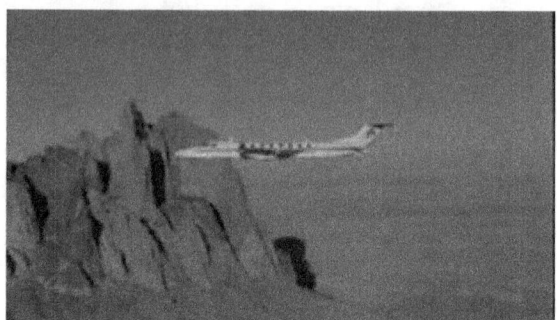

Mesa Airlines 1900C at Ship Rock NM

The photo above was using the Sony 3chip camera mounted on a specially designed swing in swing out pedestal that was designed for that aircraft to shoot out the side escape hatch when the hatch is removed.

On photo trips we usually miss breakfast because hotel restaurants don't open early enough. Then we have a late or early lunch during a refueling stop, and would not return for dinner until late. Rarely do you get to see the sites except from the air at 300 feet, working in close formation with another plane low to the ground. 300 to 3000 ft. that's my kind of flying; at 32,000ft it is just boring.

Shooting notes: I have been asked why the tough work schedule for shooting. As the producer, I have a lot of responsibility to get done as fast as I can to save money. The plane costs about $600 an hour, 35 gallons of fuel use on each engine each hour, which includes the $250 hour fuel cost. The pilot, video photographer and equipment costs $600 a day for rental. This is a special rate; normal rate for a twin engine turbo-prop is more than $2500 a day.

Add motel, food and rentals and a shoot can add up to thousands a day which are charged to the project budget. If we are shooting another plane, the costs just double. If you go over budget you better have a good reason.

Lighting Notes: I try to be up and in the air to start shooting at about 5:30 AM to take advantage of the sky conditions and color since sunrise is about 45 minuets earlier at altitude than it will be on the ground. "Magic Hour" is early sunrise to about 8:30AM and 1 hour before sundown till dark on the ground.

I have actively shot past "dark on the ground" for about 30 minutes if I can get street lights or landing lights with the plane still getting some low angle sun. Close formation in the dark will ruin your day so we open it up a bit.

The times between 10AM and 4PM were spent doing cutaways, B-Rolls, interviews, night lighting beauty shots or changing locations and planning details for the next time slots. A ground taxi shot arriving at FBO at night is usually awesome.

The next day we slept in, but still arrived at the airport by 5:00AM and setup a camera on the west end of the main runway just at the threshold (this was cleared with the tower the day before to let us on the runway).

Money shot at Mesa

At this location we captured the **"Money Shot"** of the movie. As the sun was rising over the mountains it came up right down the center line of the runway. When Tony flew the approach and landed he appeared to land into the sun, which silhouetted the aircraft, with the exhaust of the engines putting out heat waves traveling across the runway on touch down. We were shooting sound at the time and watching the shot on the monitor it was very hard not to scream OMG!

I was watching on the color monitor and saw it in color, I thought I would cry! The traffic at the time was using a crossing runway for takeoff and landings so we had to do ours between theirs. Please take a look at the 1900 video http://acfs.biz

After the take off and landing shots at Mesa, Arizona, we packed up and headed west to Page, Arizona for shots around and over Lake Powell. At Page we checked in at the motel and stowed our luggage. Up early, as normal for the film crew, we departed for Lake Powell airport and shot some early morning B-Roll with all cameras returning to Page for lunch.

The Bullfrog Basin Affair

After lunch we mounted up and tried to find the "Bullfrog Basin" airstrip in Utah, Toney's suggestion. This airstrip was very difficult to find due to it just being an unimproved dirt strip on the side of a very steep mountain near a small village on the lake.

Thank goodness we were very light and Tony, being one of the best Experimental Pilots I have flown with, is certified to fly the 1900C in experimental conditions. We landed "uphill" only to find some fairly large boulders scattered all about. During landing a few loud clunks were evident that the rocks were threw up by the tires and hit the fuselage.

As we taxied to the "high" end of the runway we also noticed that the ride was unexpectedly rough. I could only think of a damaged plane and how to explain how it happened proved to be only a minor problem.

Mike and I got out with the Sony camera and tripod and setup a camera position at the end of the runway.

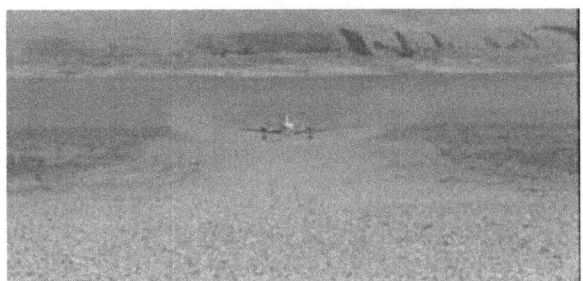

First the great shots; with Tony starting his takeoff from the low end with the lake and some mountains and lake in the background. As he spun up the engines a great plume of dust puffed up behind the 1900 and started to slowly drift with the wind.

Then, when rolling up the runway at "Rotation" he pulled up the gear and flew over our heads. And we thought that was a great shot, but wait, there was the landing to go and it proved to be even better.

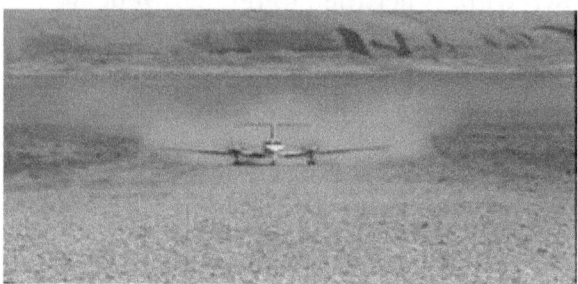

The 1900 is a big airplane for this runway, it's wing span is just over 54 feet and it can have a passenger capacity of 19 with a crew of two, so coming into and landing on this little dirt strip was awesome and I am sure we got a lot of local attention.

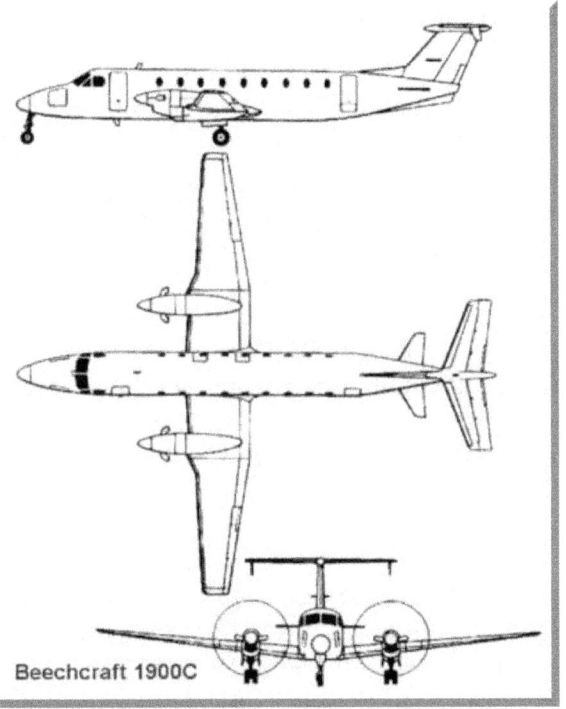

Beechcraft 1900C

You will also see in the movie the landing at Bullfrog Basin, also known as Halls Crossing, UT. It was over the top in cool shots.

The wing-tip vortices during short approach formed small wing tip vortices or horizontal tornados and started to kick up a lot of the reddish brown dirt.

While researching satellite photos for this book on Google Earth, Bullfrog Basin shows the dirt runway closed.

Gone are the rocks and dirt that once made Bullfrog Basin so exceptional for photography.

Park Rangers Arrive

Mike and I were so deeply involved in setting up and shooting the location we did not notice that a car had pulled up and two Park Rangers got out with guns drawn and everything. Many things go through your mind when the police draw down on you, being the responsible "ring leader" of this group; I could only think this could be a bad day.

Come to find out they thought we were some kind of drug smugglers landing at "their airstrip" to off load drugs. I guess they did not realize that most drug runners would not have a camera crew out to film the landing of their drug flights.

They demanded that the plane land so that they can inspect the cargo. I complied and radioed Tony to land and shut down at the high end where we were. I think I said the Park Service needed to inspect the plane, so Tony was probably a little concerned also.

This situation with a camera crew was not normal at Bullfrog airport. While one kept an eye on Mike and I, the other opened the door and proceeded to check out the internal of the plane.

I guess from their view point it looked very suspicious for a large aircraft to land over and over again at Bullfrog Basin, Utah, an airport that probably never had seen that size airplane ever.

The interior was devoid of seats being an "Experimental aircraft", nothing was found in the plane but we were not out of the woods yet. There was a small matter of not having a "Commercial Filming permit" for a U.S. Park!

None of us had any idea we would be filming in a National Park, maybe over one, but not touching the ground. Shooting for Beech / Raytheon for about 20 years I have been to every state west of the Mississippi River and flown over many Parks with no problems, till now.

The Park Rangers asked us to get in their car and travel down to the ranger station for interrogation. On the way to the ranger station I was thinking that one misstep and we could be in hot water. At the station they made us very comfortable, at least no handcuffs, and we proceeded to go over the problem and how it could be rectified.

Strange situations have occurred before, on one trip I was trusted to take care of one of our special guests, and I had allowed Mrs. Beech's grandson to go missing in East St. Louis when he was helping me with an event for the company. Luckily, before we notified the athorities, he did show up after being about 4 hours late. That is when I started to go white headed.

Back at the Bullfrog Basin Ranger Station, I found out from the rangers that the permit was "free" **however;** I would have had to send in for the license six weeks before to Washington D.C. After about an hour, which seemed like 8 to me, we came to an agreement that did not involve "incarceration" or "aircraft confiscation".

At the Ranger Station when they found that I worked for Raytheon, they came up with an idea. They wanted me to obtain a ship's radar system for their Park Ranger Boat, so they could search for missing boats in the dark. I said that I would try to convince the Raytheon Marine people to send them a unit.

I did try my best to get one for them, don't know if they ever got one, their ranger station was also included in the credits of the film to say thanks.

After they returned us to the plane we said "good by" then quickly "kicked the tires and lit the fires" and proceeded to evacuate the area at maximum speed hoping that they would not change their minds. At least we could fly quickly out of Utah. Once in the air we all started to breathe easer.

Now you know the story behind the dirt field landing shot in the film. Strange, not much was ever said among us about our run-in with the law that day.

Note: Many times you can swap inclusion in a movie for stays or other services. I swapped writing a letter instead of paying a fine and having my aircraft impounded. I should have asked Tony, who is responsible for the plane, what he thought about the affair at Bullfrog Basin but never got around to finding out.

Production Notes "The Tradition of Excellence 1900C"

The cameras used:

A Hand controlled "lipstick" cam on the belly that I could turn left or right. Because of its size this small camera had no effect on control of the aircraft which was a major concern at that time.

A Stationary "lipstick cam" mounted in the bullet of the T-tail for the wide "nacelle to nacelle" shot. This camera was cool for a POV shot showing ground terrain.

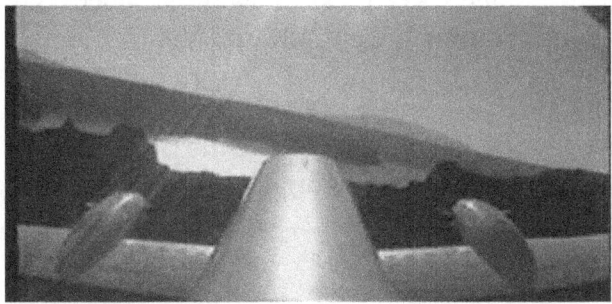

The lipstick cameras were for cutaways due to their low resolution around 400 lines and one quarter inch CCD.

By removal of the right side escape hatch before flight, we could swing a 3-chip Sony camera into the opening and shoot great starboard side "air to air" shots. We used a Beta-Cam recorder that could be dismounted from the pedestal and use on a tripod for outdoor shots.

We had a wireless Sony camera mounted wireless mike pack, used for on-camera talent interviews.

Of course the cases of tape, batteries, chargers, cables and monitors needed to check our shots added to the large amount of cargo that went along with us everywhere. Later I purchased a 24VDC to 115VAC power supply to plug-in battery chargers and charge batteries while in flight.

Note: For very early morning shots we would put the filter on Daylight with little ND (neutral density) and **NOT** press the white balance. This would preserve the extra warm color of the shot and the reason for getting up so early. When the aircraft would land over our camera into the sun then we would pop in the ND to make the plane a silhouette with the sun exposed normal. We got some great exhaust plumes from the engines against the sun.

1900 Trivia: The 1900B had a door on the left rear side of the aircraft that proved troublesome for baggage weight and balance, so they changed the rear door to a much larger cargo door, added a front passenger door ahead of the propellers and called it the model a "1900C". A few years later the model changed again when the floor to ceiling height increased to 5 feet 6 inches and called it a 1900D. I made a movie about that model change and called it "The Tradition of Excellence Continues"

"Riding the Rocket Ship"

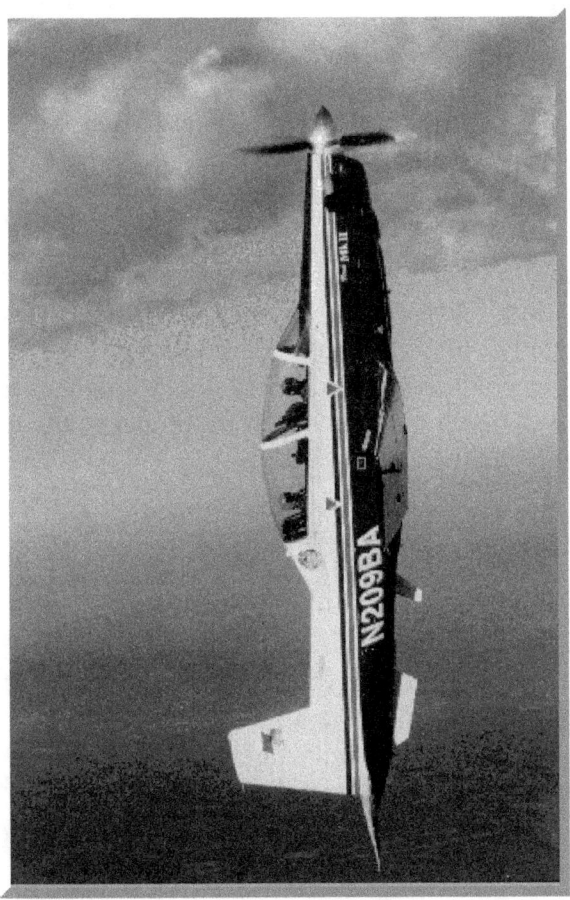

Marketing missions with new model aircraft are fun and very hard work. Beech modified the Pilatus PC-9 a single turboprop engine plane to replace the aging Beech T34C Mentor series aircraft that had been teaching Navy pilots there "Initial" training for 30 years or more.

The T-6A, Texan II as it is called, is like riding a rocket ship due to the "Thrust to Weight" ratio.

My ride in the T-6A was interesting in that this was my first "G-Suite" and was "Tied" to the ejection seat by my legs, had a mask on the helmet and was instructed to Never pull "this handle" unless instructed by the pilot.

Takeoff put you back in your seat and of course with me along we were filming in close formation with another T-6A. The picture shows a T-6A going vertical but you must remember the photo plane was doing the same thing with the photographer in the back, notice the horizon.

The footage I was doing was a test for when Patty Wagstaff would fly for a PR shoot. I met Patty at an air show I was filming at Andrews AFB, Washington D.C. Patty is a very pleasant person and fun to be around. Her roll as a "Demo Pilot" for the T-6A/B has taken her to air shows in Paris, Singapore and Farnborough England. When you are strapped in you have very little movement and to complicate even more I had a bad head cold, so this flight was not to fun.

Production Notes "T-6A"

The T-6A shooting consisted of two sections: Section One would be the Maintenance and Operation Systems where we got into great detail doing nuts and bolts. Section Two would be showing the Flight Characteristics which lead to a few days in south central Texas for a lot of formation flying for motion and stills.

The Marketing liaison came up with a shooting schedule and assignments for the four aircraft and 13 crew members to accomplish the shoot over 5 days and decided on Kerrville, Texas for terrain and weather.

I was impressed with his organization with only two small problems. Problem one, time was organized to where there was little time for breaks and fueling for both aircraft and people. Problem two, flying time with shots did not always have sun angle and lighting in mind. But over all I have never been so scheduled, usually I have a list of shots that cover a list of goals.

We accomplished a similar shot with BB-343 configured with full flaps and gear up near stall following a T-6A on landing to touch down. That shot was good but the still shot of my photo ship in that configuration and that low to the ground was awesome.

The Search for a Mystery Jet

Why the Search

For years Beech Management and Engineering was trying to come up with a jet model for the only major company that did not have one. Plan A; Designing one in-house, proved too expensive with 7 years of certification costs. Plan B; buying one on the market, but it would have to meet our quality standards.

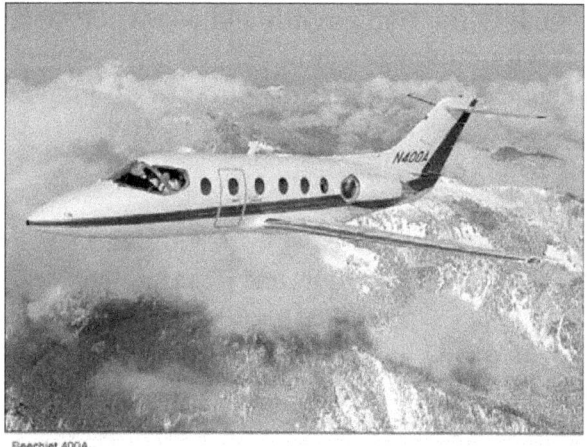

Beechjet 400A

After much consideration they found a current model that was fast, and with a solid design. Looking at the specifications this jet was better than most American jets; in fact it felt like a much larger jet, something that sold it to the Air Force to train pilots for the Tanker Training (TTS).

They also found out that this jet did have one flaw: the Japanese were good at building a product but they did not have any sales organization in America. It was easy to buy this low priced jet and make it part of the Beech product line, just one thing; how do you build it? Since Beech was playing around with jets for years they never put together the technical staff to get serious, as in their minds the King Air turboprop, was less expensive to own and operate so why have a jet. Only problem with that idea is that "Everyone else has a Jet" and to compete with Cessna and Lear we needed a Jet.

As another example of the difficulty that audio visual and photographic services faced; when the purchase of the "Beechjet" was to take place in Dallas, one of our still photographers, John Cook, was notified of an assignment he was to be prepared to photograph. He wasn't told where or when but just to be prepared, and that was all the direction he was given. No idea of whether he should wear a coat and tie or be prepared for the worst of conditions; the secrecy of the purchase was that tight, the company wanted nothing to possibly allow for a "leak" of the purchase. His professionalism gave him the insight to know that something "special" was to happen and he was prepared to record the signing of the documents of purchase.

The price was right and the deal done! After purchase, tooling was to be transferred to America and the jet was to be built at Plant IV in Wichita. But the one minor problem; assembly workers needed to know how to put together the parts.

After the first trip to Japan by management, they decided to task the people responsible for assembly to learn how to do the work. To accomplish the goal of training the staff the company needed to send manufacturing specialists and a photographer to document the process.

My good friend Don Cook asked me if I could go to Japan with about 10 manufacturing people, all of which did not speak Japanese to capture the assembly process. The trip would last about 2 weeks and provide a basis to start construction in Kansas.

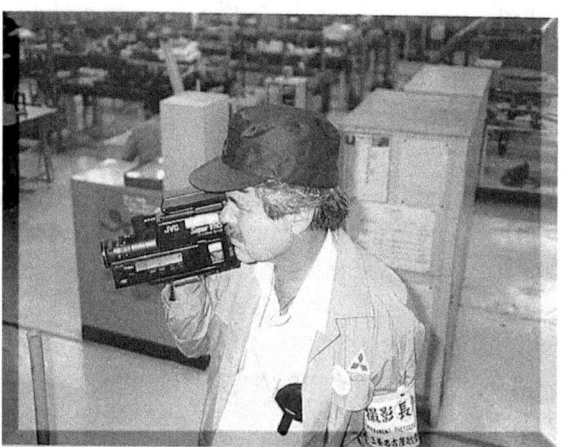

Video Filming in Japan

We documented all procedures and work flow but as a safety backup about 10 selected Japanese assembly personnel came back to America to answer questions and check our methods. Their version of assembly tooling and ours was way different, not to mention our engineers decided to change the design and add a fuel tank in the fuselage, so some of what we documented was changed before it was started in the U.S.

Culture Shock Found In Japan

Our Japanese hosts were excellent and would help us with any problems that came up. Although our orientation meetings at Beech covered a lot of ground, there were still situations that came up that were not covered. Case in point; the Japanese were big on "business Cards" they all had them and proceeded to hand them out like free passes to a Sapporo Beer Garden Party. If we had been told about this custom we would have had plenty business cards on hand to give our hosts.

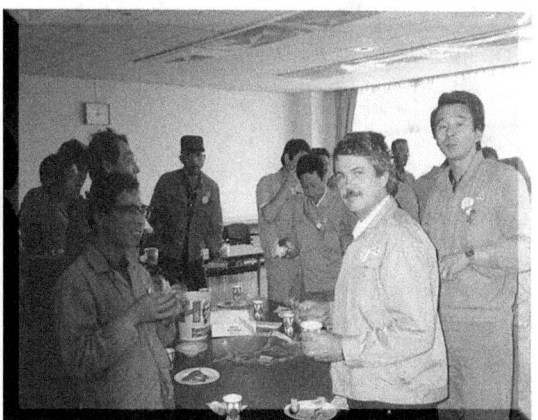
Uniforms

One other custom our orientation did not cover was that after work the Japanese management and their guests, us, would meet at a local Calamari & Kobe Steak restaurant for Sake and Karaoke until real late. I still do not remember how we got back to the hotel those nights, but I think Don and I were hits at Karaoke, they all raised their arms and said "Bonsai" wherever we went for a few days. It was a blast but next morning you felt a little used.

While in the Mitsubishi plant, we were required to wear a jacket and cap uniforms, which was a new twist as no one needed uniforms at home. We were staying in the Nagoya International Hotel, in the center of the 4th largest city in Japan, around 2 million people.

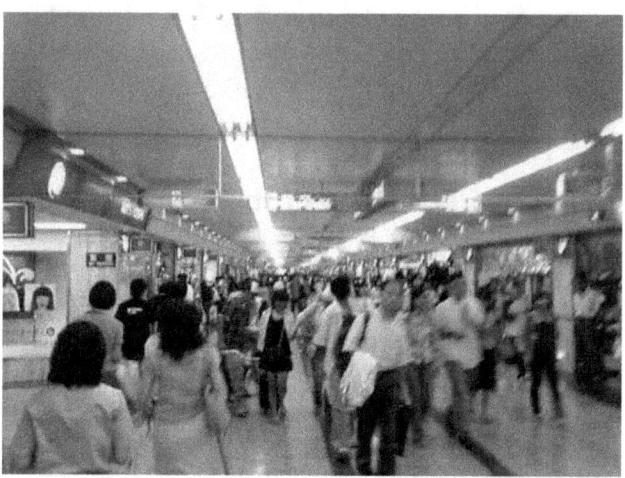

There was an "Under Ground" under the streets of Nagoya that had vendors side by side along the walls of the tunnels and the aroma of whatever they were cooking attacked my foreign sense of smell like a hammer.

I had thought that Japan would be a great place to pickup gifts for all my friends at home. Due to the exchange rate everything was too expensive and all the instructions on the products were written in Japanese, if I could not find the on button, I did not buy it.

We had to take a cab to the plant, what a ride. The hotel would call the cab and after we all got in we would hold up a piece of paper with the destination to show the driver, later paying with their funny money was another story.

This was my first experience with the left side of the road driving. The meaning of "Chaos" was driven home when left side driving in heavy traffic that included lots of bicycles and people, not having a clue where we were going, made for a morning commute that woke you up if it did not make you sick. We were not allowed to drive in Japan and I know why.

The photographer's duty was to document how the Japanese built the "Diamond Biz Jet" which when built in the United States would become a new jet model. Truly the Japanese built the aircraft in a unique way.

There each worker would be able to take a bunch of parts put in his grocery basket and build a large section of the airplane. Here a group of workers would build "their small part" of a subassembly and none of the people knew how to do it all.

The Japanese had one interesting manufacturing procedure. When moving a large piece such as a wing assembly everyone put on their hard hats and the leader would blow a whistle in some kind of code almost continually as the assembly was hoisted and moved to its new location.

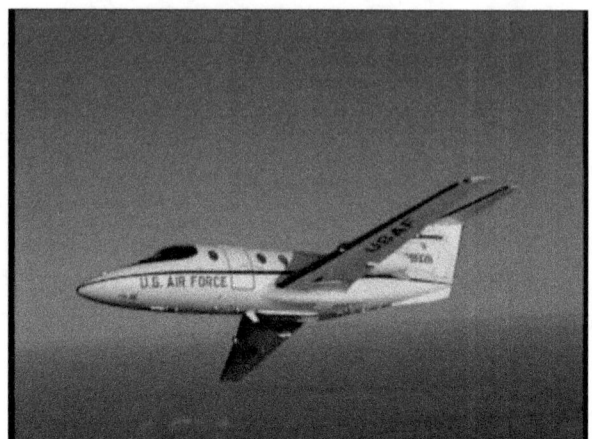

T-1A, US Air Force Version of a Beechjet

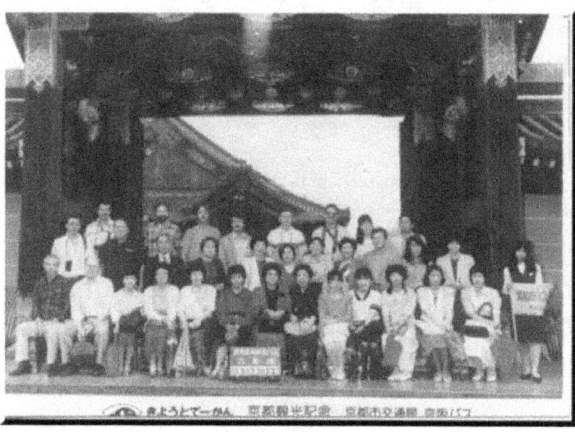

The upside was that we had the weekend to sightsee, something industrial photographers infrequently get to do, but it rained. We usually take pictures of other people sightseeing. However, this time we got to see the Nagoya Castle, Bullet Train to Kyoto and the Shrine of Fertility. I still don't get it; there were men, women and children running around praying and buying icons of the male parts to take home.

Back home our marketing department held a "big contest" to come up with a hot "American" name for our first commercial jet in the company's history. The prize money was considerable and the hype of the decision selection game was played to the hilt.

After hundreds or maybe thousands of suggestions they announced the name "Beechjet". It was so anticlimactic and most thought it was rigged. Marketing must have been playing games; "Company Name "+"Jet" how original.

Mitsubishi Diamond Construction

I used a JVC SVHS-C camcorder where the "S" denoted that it had Super resolution. The SVHS actually recorded the video differently than the standard VHS. The "S" took the color output from the camera and split the signal into "Chroma" and "luminance", then recorded each signal consecutively strips on a chrome type tape. When played back the two signals were recombined to form a higher quality color signal.

The Standard VHS had a "composite" signal that produced "artifacts" when recorded. The artifact of composite led to things like suites or dresses that people wore looking alive and becoming a distracting herring bone light show.

Splitting the chroma off from the luminance channel kept the image sharper and cleaner on its path to your TV.

The last flight of India Foxtrot Oscar

21

The Trip That Would Not End

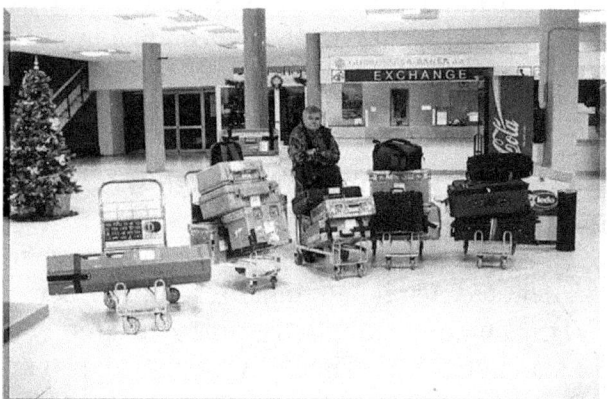
Waiting for Customs in Dubrovnik 11PM local

The one down side of being a movie crew is herding all the stuff where ever you go. On this trip overseas two of us, Mike Barnes and I had 27 heavy metal clad cases that needed to travel with us through Customs, airport connections and ground transportation.

We learned that when on the road you need to take along duplicate cords, tape, cameras and monitors packed in different cases so if one got lost it would not shut you down.

After flying from Cincinnati, Ohio to Frankfurt, Germany then to Zagreb and finally to Dubrovnik Croatia it was close to a 23 hour trip.

When in Frankfurt we were preparing to push off and the door was closed when I was setting on the window side and discovered all of our equipment was setting on the ramp and had not been loaded. Mike notified the attendant and the thoughtful pilot waited till all equipment was loaded. We were meeting the defense attorneys and investigation specialists the next day in Dubrovnik and it would have been very bad not to be ready to go.

When we arrived in Zagreb from Frankfort it was overcast and dreary just as you would expect from watching old Eastern Block films made behind the "Iron Curtain". But when we left Zagreb for Dubrovnik we were the only two people in First Class but the Coach was full. Talk about service, First Class had two Stewardesses while the Coach with all the other people had only one. When we traveled for the attorneys we always went first class.

We thought our troubles were over when we finally arrived in Dubrovnik but a host of seven Customs agents speaking broken English started giving us problems getting the equipment checked through. It was after midnight in Dubrovnik and we were the only ones left in the airport.

After out lasting the Customs people arguing about every little thing. Mike called the hotel for the car came which showed up and off to the hotel about 40 miles away.

Mike and I were toast and slept in till the next afternoon. All this time we were schlepping around about 500 lbs of cases and equipment.

Conspiracy – The investigation of an accident

The official weather report issued at the time of the crash reported light scattered rain, broken clouds at 400 feet, a thin overcast at 2000 feet, and a steady head wind right down the runway just the way pilots like it. The reported visibility was 5 miles.

The flight crew acknowledged receiving this weather report. The distance from the airport to where the aircraft crashed was less than two miles. The mountains were obscured by the broken clouds and overcast.

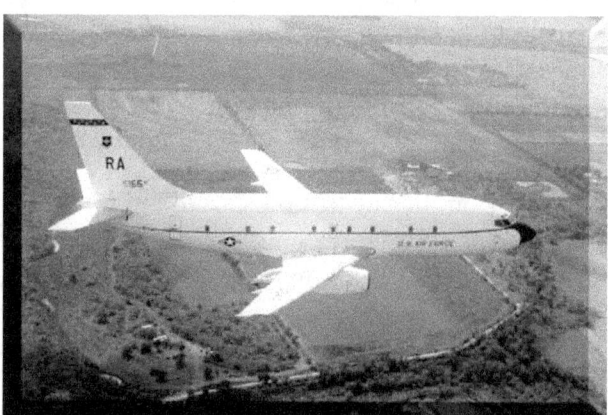

Air Force T43A (Boeing 737A)

According to Aviation Week and Space Technology, April 8, 1996, the Dubrovnik tower lost voice radio contact with the aircraft at the same time the aircraft vanished from the screens of the approach radar at Split and an AWACS aircraft.

The Split radar watches the approach to Dubrovnik airport, which is where the Ron Brown aircraft was when it dropped off of the radar screen. Contrary to some silly claims made in the media, the plane was NOT flying in the mountains.

It was actually out over the water, with open space all around. The radar at Split routinely tracks aircraft through that airspace without problem. If it were normal for the Split radar to lose traffic at that point on the approach path nobody would have mentioned it because it would be expected behavior. There would be nothing unusual about it.

That a comment was made about the target dropping off of the Split radar establishes that it was an unusual event. Why the error in flight path was not relayed to the aircraft and corrected by ground control is still a mystery.

The Split radar, like all ATC radar, tracks primarily by aircraft transponder. So, when the Split radar lost track of the Ron Brown aircraft, what was actually lost was the transponder return, as the aircraft was still there, on the approach path, although just starting to veer slightly left.

Camera Location "CV"

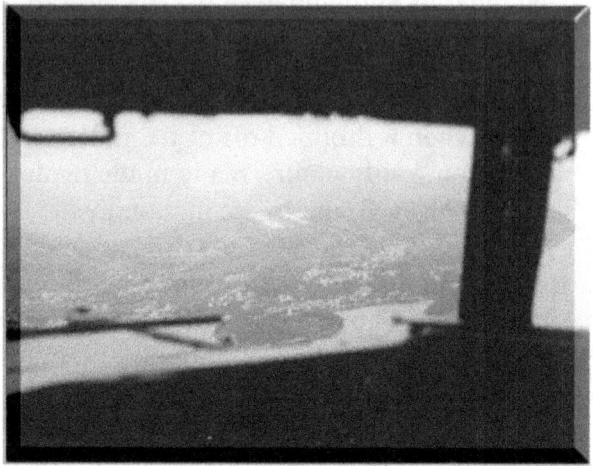

Camera Position CV – Bottom center of
Window
Dubrovnik Airport – Center of Window
Viewed through B737 Cockpit

"CV" was the NDB located on a peninsula off
Cavtat Croatia: I was to video the NDB approach
from over the peninsula of Lokrum near Dubrovnik
Airport under different scenarios. The team leased
a Boeing 737A from an airline in France and flew
different approaches for data points to be combined
later in the edit room at Dublin, Ohio.

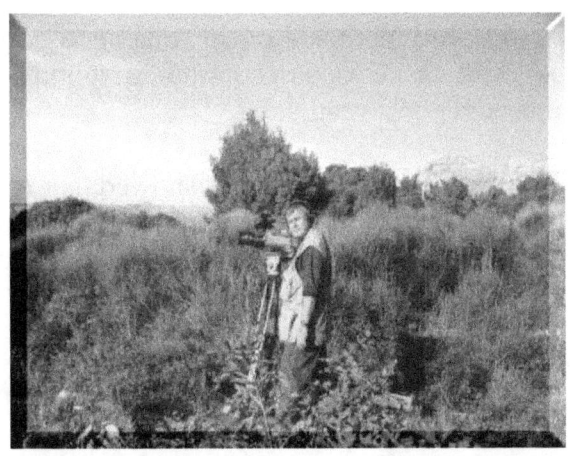

"Outstanding in my Field" at "CV" Non
Directional Beacon

Besides normal camera, tripod and video
recorder the special equipment was a satellite
phone. The first unit director, my good friend Mike
Barnes, would warn to start then about 15 seconds
mark take and a start clap that would be picked up
on the audio track for later sync in Dublin, OH
studio.

The Accident

The ADF was an onboard device that finds and
provides a pointer to a low frequency NDB or Non
Directional Beacon, developed and patented in the
1900"s. The system was the state of the art until
replaced with the VOR system in the 1960"s.

What we found did NOT have any "smoking
gun" of any conspiracy, but just a very tragic event.
The crash was after a very long day of flying from

Zagreb to Dubrovnik taking many detours trying to stay out of hot zones due to continuing fighting with the Serbs and poor weather.

Raw data from our findings showed that ADF was set **one mark off** "10 degrees" to the port side, left, which would take the plane into the mountains where it crashed instead of the airport.

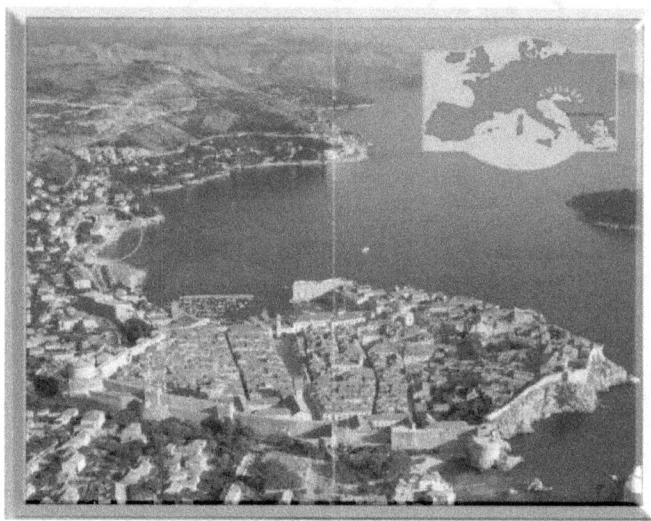

City of Dubrovnik close to the Approach of aircraft

The T43A would have flown over Dubrovnik into the clouds en route to the airport about 20 miles ahead and to the left a few degrees of the airport. The airport would be located under the inset map in the upper right side of the picture. The actual flight was more the direction of the crease in the picture which ended tragically in the mountains east of the airport.

My interpreter was Mato Begovic, pronounced like "Meto". He was basically assigned to keep me company and be the interface with any "locals" we encountered. Pictured standing next to the NDB-CV located on a peninsula off Cavtat Croatia.

I believe that Mato's brother may have been wounded during the recent Yugoslav (YPA) war. The war got within a few miles of Dubrovnik but was stopped.

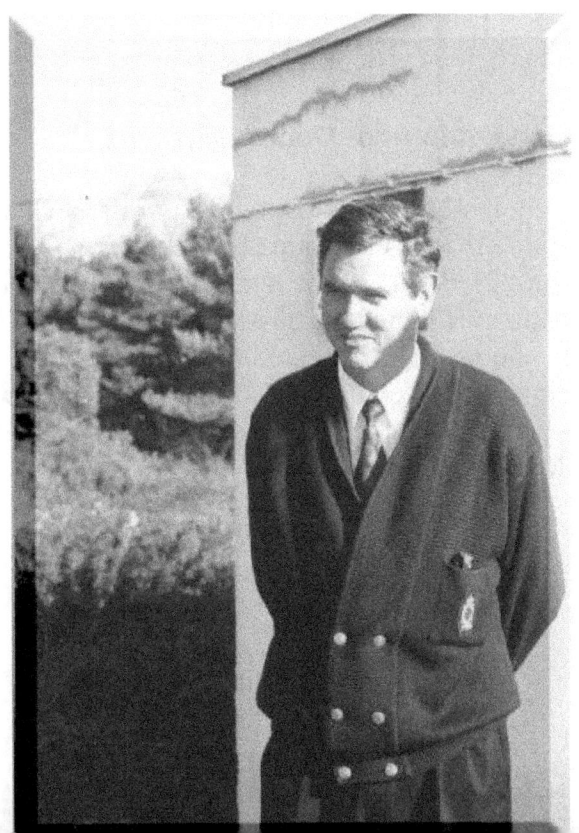

On June 25, 1991 Slovenia and Croatia declared independence from Yugoslavia. In August the battle of Vukovar began. This was the biggest battle in the War in Croatia after Oluja and Bljesak operations. In this battle 90% of the city was destroyed. YPA used fighter and attack aircraft, rocket launchers, large amount of tanks and other equipment. In October Vukovar was captured and 80% of Croatian forces were destroyed or captured.

At the same time in mid October Yugoslav ground army supported by navy and air force attacked the city of Dubrovnik and Konavle area where Ustase had their strongholds. By December 6th YPA has neutralized all Ustase formations in Konavle area but the city of Dubrovnik was not captured. After these two big operations YPA signed a peace treaty with Croatia and started to withdraw. The last YPA soldier left Croatia in May 1992.

Stolen Equipment Dooms Aircraft!

Stolen Equipment Dooms Aircraft is what the headline should have said about the India Oscar Foxtrot 21 flight. As the last Bosnian solders left Croatia they looted the airport at Dubrovnik where they unbolted and removed the one piece of equipment that could have saved the Ron Brown party 4 years later. What they took was a system called a VOR.

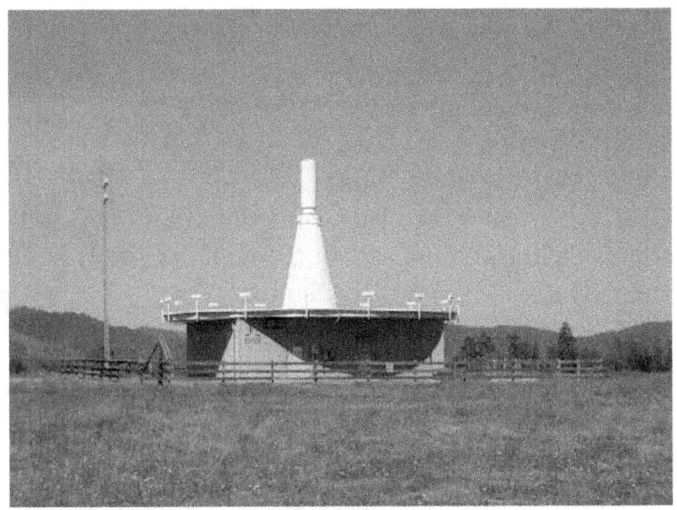

The VOR is a navigation transmitter used world wide, located at the airport, to provide a directional beacon signal to the aircraft to allow the aircraft to fly directly to the airport. The missing equipment doomed the Boeing 737 to use a much older form of navigation that had a much greater error factor and took the aircraft into the mountains.

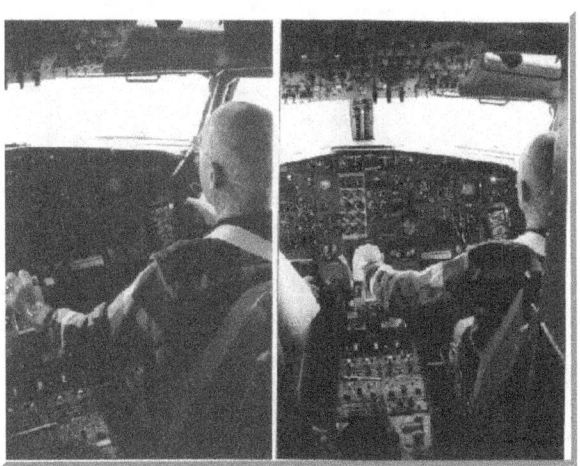

Interior B737A with Accident Investigation Team member "General Orin Godsey"

Our Team had to "Fly" the different flight scenarios to be considered expert witnesses. We had and flew the aircraft for 2 full days with a French flight crew and two flight attendants required for the flight. Mike and I were on one flight and spent most of the time talking to the flight attendants and moving about the cabin of the B737 checking audio pickups for the recording.

The Secret Starship First Flight

This operation was fun, when I told my immediate supervisor that I was going to be at work but I was not coming in tomorrow, he ask me why and I had to tell him; that I could not tell him. I was working on a special project with Linden Blue, the CEO of the company. Whatever Linden wanted, Linden got no questions.

Over the few years that Linden was at the company, I had developed a great respect for his visions of the future and he would call on me to do his special AV projects.

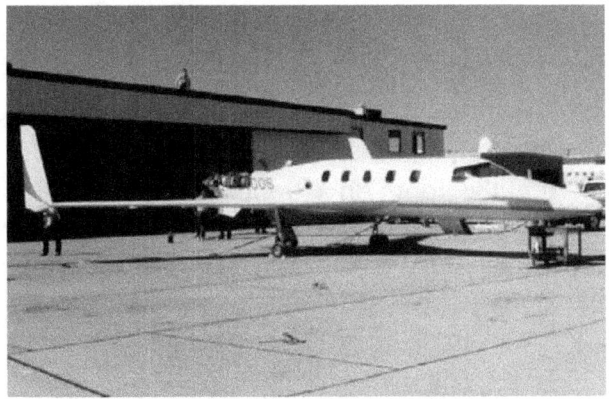

N2000S Getting Ready for the First Flight
I shot some pictures from the hanger roof on
Rollout

4 Vice President's and their wives all boarded two King Airs at 0400 hours, in the dark, and spent about 3 hours flying non-stop to the Scaled Composites in the Mojave Desert.

In preparation for Starship flight, Burt Rutan, Clay Lacy, Doug Allen and I were just a few of the members at the "pre flight" coordination meeting.

At the event I shot the all important takeoff then we raced for the Photo plane for the Air to Air.

Shooting the first flight was a blast; I was in a King Air 200 along with the CEO of Beech Aircraft and his boss, the corporate CEO of Raytheon. We took turns looking and shooting out the removed escape hatch capturing air to air of this moment in aviation history.

Video I took on the ground and in the air was quickly edited when I got back to Beech.

"Star" of the Show

Video I shot at the NBAA meeting in Dallas when the Starship flew over on the first day was shown in the booth on a "loop" in raw un-edited condition the rest of the show. The crowd was 5 people deep most of the next 4 days at the show. That many people so interested in what you shot; very rewarding.

See the raw footage and NBAA film that was used for the introduction of the Starship at the NBAA along with special music composed just for the Starship event.

"Starship Down"

The U.S. may have "Roswell" event but Denmark has the "Roskilde" Starship event.

This was an incident where one winter a Starship, was loaded with passengers and also had a load of ice on the wings when he took off, he gained a little altitude and then settled back to the ground off the runway. After the crash, there were no injuries due to the Starship's composite strength, or any loss except for the belly delaminating and some wheel well structure work. The passengers did not even have bumps or burses.

A crew of composite repair specialists and I flew to Denmark to document the repair.

I was impressed about how easy the Starship could be repaired in the field. I was only around metal aircraft for many years and when a metal aircraft has damage there is a lot of drilling, cutting and riveting involved in reconstruction.

Around a Starship that is being repaired it is "quite" with little drilling and no riveting and a faint tapping only.

First, the technician, using a very small hammer, taps his way around any damage and listens for a change in the sound. After finding a thud sound he then marks the location with a grease pencil. This delamination area is then cut out with a saw and the process for bonding in new ply's of composite weave starts.

Successful repairs can be identified by the tap method and once passing quality control moves on to paint.

I got to fly in a Starship and was amazed on how the ride was quite and comfortable. Of course for me, I was impressed about how it would make a great camera platform. Overall the normal bumps of flying were replaced with a gentle up and down motion because the composite wings would absorb most of the bumps. It was weird, you look out at the wing and it would flex a little when it hit a bump. I would fly in one every chance I got. Usually the ones I got to fly in did not have an interior, but hey that is alright.

Starship Certified to Make History

The video "**Starship Certified to Make History**" was designed to educate people on the Starships manufacturing status. This was made after the projected certification date was repeatedly extended due to snags in manufacturing, sound familiar? Construction certification delays of the Boeing 787 Dreamliner, a composite aircraft, are reminiscent of the extra time it took Starship to be certified.

The Starship is a great plane and pilots familiar with the aircraft lament the decision to scrap a large amount of the production run and stop production of new units. I always thought that if there were a "Starship II" would have small fanjets.

The Starship was the first commercial full composite aircraft. They should have been saved like the Wright Flyer, the first in powered flight. **Now I count myself very lucky to have been associated with Starship I from design to testing, to flight.**

There are very few that escaped the scrap yard, most notable to be saved is Starship NC-51 owned by my friend Robert Scherer (N514RS) who I hope to meet one day and discuss his use of NC-51.

The "Starship Certified" video won a "Silver Screen" award at the "Industrial Film and Video festival" for "Industrial Technical Process". The video can be found at http://acfs.biz with additional comments.

ASTROVISION by Clay Lacy

I met Clay several times when doing air to air, and I will be the first to say that the Lear Jet's ASTROVISION filming product is fantastic. The pilot, Clay Lacy, is excellent to say the least.

The Astrovision would shoot in 35MM film which was costly but made beautiful shots. Air to air with Clay could set you back more than $20,000 a **day** not counting the cost of the subject aircraft. It is a testament to Clay Lacey's ability that he could put his Lear Jet in the correct special position to shoot excellent shots by just using a small TV in the cockpit.

Remember he did not have a zoom lens to adjust his shots; he had to position his Lear to get them. His expertise in air to air shots can be seen in Top Gun, Flight of the Intruder and Firefox.

The Lear Jet 23 was very cramped when you added the Astrovision system in the cabin. The shooting crew consisted of an assistant who had to work around the camera to pass new magazines of film to the photographer, my friend J. Douglas Allen.

All in all, I had much more room in my King Air than Doug in the Lear Jet. I could even get up and move around after setting for long spells. Doug Allen was somewhat locked in when the airplane was in flight.

Doug Allen did shoot some excellent footage of not only the Starship but King Airs and our Jets. I met Doug in Hollywood for a few days when we were transferring film from his account at the lab to my account for safekeeping.

The first time I got to look inside the Lear jet was when we both showed up on the Secrete "Starship Prof of Concept First Flight" in 1983 in the Mojave Desert at Burt Rutan's Scaled Composites Hanger.

Burt's group built the first Starship out of fiberglass to an 85% scale. Burt was also responsible for the "Long-EZ" and Virgin Galactic "Space Ship Two" designs.

VECTORVISION by Bob Nettmann

I met with Bob Nettmann in Burbank on a shoot to discuss working on a deal to fit my Experimental King Air with an improved camera system he designed called a VECTORVISION. He could market outside with a photo ship and Beech could use on in house productions when not in use. Vectorvision had "variable zoom" capabilities which Astrovision could not do with a "fixed" lens.

Bob Nettmann was the optical whiz that invented the Astrovision system that Clay Lacy uses. In the Astrovision system you have a two axis system that has a fixed focal length lens. The Vectorvision system added a variable focal (Zoom) length lens that could also be adjusted to level the shot with the horizon. The extra adjustments made this system very usable when added to a video camera. The good thing about it is that the camera is located in the cabin and not out in the weather like my system.

SHOTMAKER by Hal Needham

I was also in talks with stuntman / director Hal Needham of "Smoky and the Bandit" fame in Atlanta in 1996 about using his "Shotmaker Truck" to film a takeoff and taxi on one of our marketing planes. Problems developed when a scheduled shoot was postponed for a couple of weeks and the window of opportunity to get the "Shotmaker" on location for the shoot closed.

Just as well, after checking the takeoff and landing speed of the Starship, I found that the Shotmaker would be past the trucks maximum speed and the runway would have to be very wide to safely accommodate both the truck and the airplane at 100+ mph.

An accident with the truck would take out the airplane and crew in a split second. However, I still dream about the shot, starting at brake release to lift off you could have a continuous shot. With a UAV now you would come close to such a shot and much safer. I have seen the use of a camera mount in front of what looks like an Apache attack helicopter with excellent results from hover stop to takeoff of light aircraft.

Designing the Camera System

The biggest problem when shooting Air to Air is shooting through Plexiglas. Shots can be distorted if the window has any curve and reflections off of the inside of the glass will ruin the shot.

Cheap Solution: We have taped a black cloth on the headliner from back to front down the center of the cabin, and get on the dark side to shoot without reflections in the Plexiglas.

Some industrial photography jobs may allow for some creativeness to solve a problem.

My advice is to be creative and come up with a solution to the problem and then present the idea with the cost and savings to your management.

It is very important to justify any costs with future savings if you expect the idea to be accepted. Your manager may not tell you of extra moneys to spend unless you ask.

Many times I would work a problem with success for both me and my manager's benefit. I would usually not design a system for any reward except to make my job easer and usually if my job was easer my output was better and everyone is happy.

Beech Vision Shooting Strategies

I designed an aerial camera system saved money the first time it was used. An Experimental Model 200 (Serial BB-343) was modified to develop the updated Collins systems to be used on the newer King Air model 300 and flew in this configuration on October 6, 1981.

After returning to Beech and the removal of the advanced KA300 avionics package, BB-343 was fitted with whatever avionics and instruments were lying around, literally. The Autopilot was never reinstalled. The "Yaw Dampener" was missing, so the pilot had to "hand fly" the aircraft 100% of the time.

At altitude it would gently swing left and right a few degrees, which tended to put you asleep if

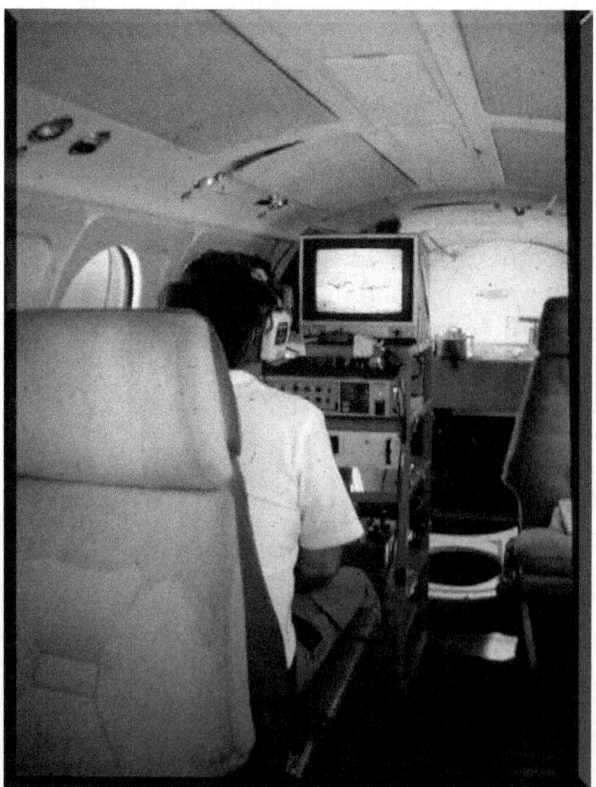

you were in the back but it was a camera shooters nightmare at altitude.

Due to the missing Autopilot, I had the opportunity to fly a lot of "Right Seat Time" to spell the pilot on long trips. I spent many a days in this airplane on photo missions.

The lack of a Yaw Dampener made some close-ups shots out of the question.

My original camera design had two parts; one was the faring located between the bottom of the fuselage to the point where the pan / tilt would move and the camera enclosure. Think of the camera enclosure part as an upside down rounded trash basket with a slit cut in one side where the lens protruded.

After the second flight I "Trashed the trash can", it induced tremendous vibration to the camera and the pilot said it added a sloppy feel to the rudder.

With the camera hanging out in the 300mph slip stream we had to be careful not to fly through rain or ice. The camera held up surprisingly well with little vibration. The only difficulty was panning past 90 degree left or right. The lens provided ample drag to over power the servo motors.

When ever I needed to shoot forward the pilot could decrease the airspeed to about 100mph and the pan motor would allow me to move the camera forward, and then back to cruse speed. Many times I would point the camera straight down, pan forward and then pull the camera up to a forward position.

When the camera was pointing directly in trail it would produce awesome pictures like the shot of a King Air skimming the tops of clouds that I shot over the coast of Oregon when the low sun angle was about 1 hour from sunset.

Test Videos of most all Flight Test Aircraft, like the Beechjet, the Starship, the 1900, Single and Twin engines and the "Special Mission" aircraft were everyday occurrences using our own aircraft. I must note that the pilots are highly qualified flight test personnel, but they are not photographers.

When shooting from the cabin door the exhaust gases from the left engine made the shot fuzzy so the only thing to do was to have the pilot shut down the left engine during filming.

This was a little dangerous due to the altitude that most of the shots were at was only 1,000 feet above the water. Here is where you had to have total trust in the pilot being able to control the plane. One hiccup from the engine at 1,000 feet over the Gulf of Mexico would spoil your day.

Whenever we remove the cabin door to shoot the right side of the subject aircraft, the photographer needed to be "safety belted" in so he would not fall out. This always made me wonder, if someone did fall out the door, I would not have enough strength to pull him back in the door against a too hundred mile per hour wind. I did not have a tether so if I went to pull him in could I fall out?

Usually the still photographer would be seated on the floor just out of the slip stream on the inside of the aircraft. Difference of wind velocity was whipping from 150 MPH in the cabin to over a solid 300 MPH just outside of the door.

If you were not careful, your camera could get caught in the high speed wind and be ripped out of your hand in a fraction of a second. If something did go out while in formation, would it hurt the subject plane? We needed to check the aircraft before flight for any loose items that would be sucked out of the gaping door.

The still photographer was always in complete agreement with me when it was suggested that he be "belted' in and he confided in me that he too doubted my ability to "haul" him back in if he did indeed "fall" out of the aircraft.

He commented to me the while the open doorway provided a great "window" to shoot out of if shooting straight out or to the rear quarter of sight line, the inability to see things coming because of vision being blocked by the width of the wing did cause some problems.

After about two hours of shooting, I had to break it off and have all aircraft returned to Port Author because everyone was very tired and we did not want to push anyone too far as an accident could ruin everyone's day.

"Will Record"

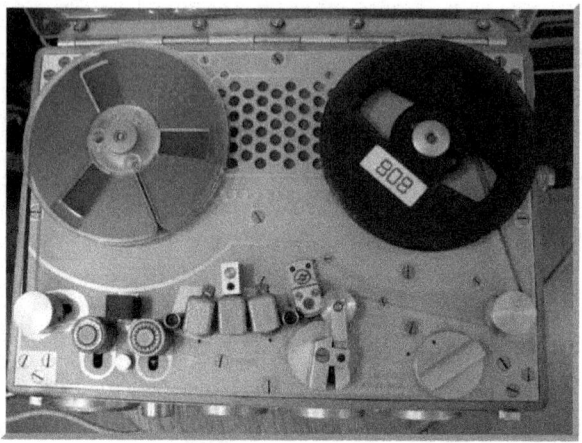

Nagra III which means "Will Record, III version" in Polish was really made in Switzerland and holds 12 "D" size batteries, and becomes very heavy lugging it around with the shoulder strap. On the leather case flap / lid I had a couple of pieces of webbing sowed on to hold the earphones that were specially made for the recorder, thus freeing up a hand during changing locations.

The Nagra series used 1/4" reel to reel tape and the one I used was set to run at 7.5" per second. As noted on the picture the round objects on each side are tension rollers.

From the left side the next two rollers push the tape up to the erase head, the black square. The next in the tape path is a guide to position the tape on the next three heads, grey rounded squares. The Left head was the Record head the middle head is the "Pilot" head that lays the 60 cycle tone in the center of the tape and the right head is the Playback head. Next in line is the exit tape guide followed by the Capstan and Pinch Roller. Next to the right tension roller is the Control knob.

Turning the control knob all the way counter clock wise will put the deck into "Rewind".

- Turning it to "Match the dots" will NOT engage the pinch roller and put the deck in Pause.

- Turning the knob to the extreme right WILL engage the pinch roller and put the deck in Record or Play. (pictured)

Why our pilots were so good

Our pilots for any trips that we used camera aircraft all came from the "Experimental Flight Test" department. Each pilot had thousands of hours flying our planes. They were the "Elite" of all company pilots. All were certified every few months for close formation work so I had no problems putting my life in their hands. I can't say enough about the pilots, they only wore parachutes if they were taking an aircraft beyond its certified limits or close to the failure limit.

There was one time when I went aboard requesting a chute because we were trying to duplicate an accident in a King Air where eight people died during an icing condition near Chicago. It was my feeling that a chute would be necessary if we were successful in duplicating the incident but my pilot said don't worry, I don't have a chute. I was not sure if that was good or bad that he did not have a chute. As it turned out the loss of control did not happen no matter how hard we tried to duplicate the condition.

When we used "Other Pilots"

A Bonanza movie I worked on in Florida I was in the #4 aircraft in a left echelon flight of 4 aircraft that went from Opa-Locka (described above), close to Miami, to a little strip on Key Largo. Note you cannot find the Key Largo airport now, it is a bunch high priced houses.

My pilot, #4 ship, we hired locally to fly the forth plane, was not formation qualified and it showed in formation. He was all over the sky not even visually locked to the #3 aircraft like he should.

I felt that he would have a mid-air with #3 and the question in my mind was; would the crash kill me or would I drown after I hit and the sharks in the water below in Biscayne Bay do me in?

The outside position is the hardest one because you are farthest from the photo aircraft and any movement is magnified. Consider that the #1 position will vary plus or minus 5 feet compared to the photo ship due to wind turbulence. Now ship #2 will try to lock on #1s movement and will be a delayed movement plus or minus 5 feet compared to #1. Now #3 will move another 5 feet trying to follow #2 you can imagine that #4 would be moving40 feet up or down most of the time.

Visually from the photo ship the other aircraft looked more like a whip moving up and down. In the still world, a photographer could stop the motion and make a decent picture, but movies show "Time".

This Air to Air was so bad we could not use any shots, and I was so scared of that pilot's skills, I never got back on his airplane and drove back to Miami with Bob and the equipment. We should never have tried a 4 ship shot.

Shooting Note: Propeller Planes and Library Archives

For prop planes, never use shutter speeds beyond 1/120 second unless it is for non-marketing photos. When the props stop is looks like an old WWII gun camera shots, very amateur.

When shooting with movie film, props blur, not a factor if speeds stay at 24 fps (Sound Speed). I quickly learned that shooting "Everything" as though it was Marketing Quality, I would have all kinds of shots that I would use in marketing videos. Because scripts called for engineering shots in marketing films it would be "in the can" and I could use it at a moments notice. Building videos with different categories of shots would be the basis of many Quick turnaround Public Relations flicks.

With an extensive library of marketing, engineering and manufacturing shots, a 5 to 10 minute company product and facilities video was easy, just chop some shots together and add music, titles and narration. Using NLE, Non Liner Editor such as a Fast Video Machine or Final Cut Pro would make the job much easer than the old way of Liner editing ¾ inch or 1 inch.

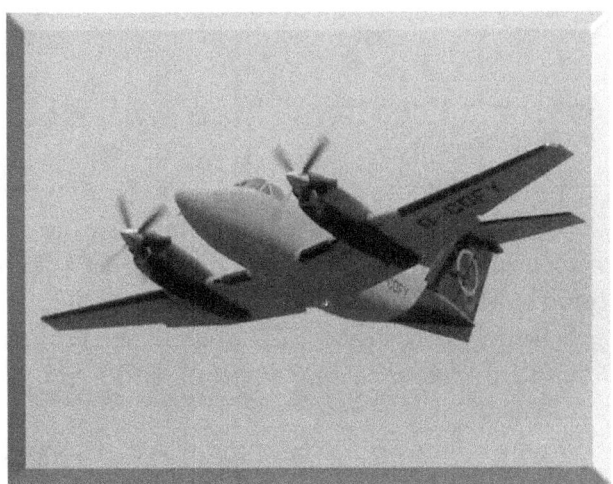

Stopping Props is a No-No

Making a Creative Video with NLE

In the early days we would go to Hollywood CA to CFI or Consolidated Film Industries to oversee final editing of 16mm films. Glen Glenn Sound studios were part of CFI, but with the decrease in film usage CFI is now a vacant lot and Glen Glenn Sound is now a part of Todd-AO.

Later I would go to Burbank CA to Compact Video to do final edits of productions on their 1 inch multi-deck studios. I would have to sometimes wait until very late at night to get time at Compact, which was located in back of NBC studios.

My editor also did "Married with Children". Later after my NLE was setup, I did not need to pack my tapes and fly to the studios, but I would at times spend a few 18 hour days in my edit bay to finish a project after the phone stops ringing.

Using a NLE is fast if you are organized, the first thing you do is digitize all production tapes that you have marked as scenes you need to include in the project. Important, always lay 30 seconds on head and tail of all shots to provide slop that will save you time if the selected shot is too short to cover the narration.

I would start by laying an "Audio" track with the Narration. Next I would lay the "Title / Open" sequence followed by the digitized shots to match the audio track. After all shots are laid, then add the Titles and Credits and any special visual effects.

After the basic video and narration, the next track is the special sound effects and music tracks. Since the number of films and videos that I made, I would setup an annual lease on my music library that would cover all needle drops used. A list of Needle drops for each production needed to be sent to the record library to establish clearance of music.

Over the years I would change the music library to keep the sound fresh for the movie era. I used Capitol, KPM and DeWolf in the later years.

When all is down it is time to run the full video and judge the composite product. If the video "feels" right, then call in the "requestor" and get his input. Any changes can be made easily using the NLE at this point.

Only thing left after approval is to digitally master the video for distribution.

I had built a rack of 10 VHS and 3 Betamax recorders that I could use to duplicate too from master tapes. Also since we would get requests from international users I had 2 VHS recorders that would do PAL / SECAM. I would get high grade tapes from a local distributor in bulk with no box or labels. Orders of 100 units can be filled in a day that included foreign standards.

The switcher that I designed could monitor all recorders for quality control purposes and verify proper signals went to the recorders. I was using three Panasonic MII for editing and one BetaCam recorder / player to feed both NLE bays and the duplicating racks.

How to stay away from the Feds

Not all Industrial Photography jobs are that exciting but all are demanding in their own way. We did set limitations to our air to air; locations west of the Mississippi River were easy to shoot as the air traffic was light below 23,000ft.

East of the Mississippi River was much more crowded with air traffic and was dense even at lower altitudes. We found it much easer to mistakenly violate some F.A.R. (Federal Aviation Regulations) in the eastern US.

Flying Low and Fast

To show the airplane with great backgrounds we had to fly low and in close formation. Low and close flying demonstrated "Speed" where shooting high altitude was boring. Showing an aircraft high above the clouds, normally where you would find them, was not as interesting. The only exception to unexciting high altitude shooting was if we could fly just over cloud tops or show cloud penetration at cruse speed.

We found that shooting along the Gulf Coast and most of Florida was productive except if we got too close to the U.S. boarder, they always thought we were running drugs.

Over Ambitious Photo Shoots

The most ambitious photo shoot was for our marketing department, and was crippled from the start. The shoot involved 4 aircraft with 7 pilots, Talent, a crew of 6 and was scheduled to start on a Saturday morning and end on Sunday evening, returning to Wichita for work Monday. This was the only time I could get all aircraft at once and still have time to edit.

The aircraft involved were The Starship I, BeechJet, King Air 350 and my King Air photo ship; BB-343. We propositioned our group in Eugene Organ on Friday for early shooting the next day; with ground work in McMinnville Organ we basically took over the airport for a day.

I tasked Mike to recreate the "Incomparable Baron Open" shot. The speed dynamics of a "Starship" landing and the white color of the airplane, instead of dark blue of the Kitty Hawk Baron, made the shot very complex. The Starship needed a lot more runway length to be safe.

Because we had to "Airline" Brockman from Greensboro, NC out to Wichita, in time to fly him with us to McMinnville, Oregon also made the logistics distracting from the video setup.

This was one of the times it became overwhelming and I decided to not do it that away again. It was my fault, I spread myself to thin letting assistant director do the shots with Brockman. This was a time when we tried to do too much with too many over a short weekend.

What I needed to do was get an assistant to do the logistics and coordination work, and I should have been on the ground directing the talent and aircraft. The difficulty arose because only I was proficient with the airborne camera system and needed to be in BB-343.

Engineering High Speed Tests

(**From Doug Ambler**) Occasionally our engineering department would request slow motion studies including landing gear drop tests and fuselage drop tests involving a crash dummy wired to the max with sensors. To achieve slow motion, the camera has to be over-cranked from its normal 24 frames per second (FPS).

For example, a modest 100 FPS cuts the light falling on the film four times. For extreme high speed we used a HYCAM with a rotating prism shutter that could shoot up to 10,000 FPS. I stopped at 1,000 FPS because of the need for extremely bright lights to expose the film properly. Engineering had a power cart made up to power 20-1,000 watt quartz halogen lights.

I couldn't leave them on very long because it would start smoking the surface of the subject due to the extreme heat. I learned this when I noticed a wisp of smoke from the crash test dummy when I was getting a light reading.

High Speed Filming / Slow Motion

An example of "Over or Under Cranking a camera" is in the late 1980's and early 1990's when high speed video was not yet a viable option for some engineering tests, so you had to shoot in film with hi-speed cameras to capture an event and then transfer only the part you needed for video. One example is doing a landing gear drop, shot in high speed running through 400 feet of film at 2,000FPS, but the event it's self can be transferred for later viewing of the event in video. Did you ever sit through 10 minutes of anything waiting for the 5 seconds of action?

Shooting propeller aircraft at over 100fps will start to stop propellers, very amateur. If we stopped a propeller for a marketing film we would get "read the riot act".

Terms and Specifications for Film Equipment

Old School Photographer

We had a photographer, Frank Madson, that was called "Just One More", he was old school and shot with a 4x5 Speed Graphic and flash bulbs; this was the camera used in the 1930's into the 1960's and exposed a huge 4 inch by 5 inch piece of "sheet film". The quality was excellent since with that size film most prints could be "Contact Prints" with no enlarger needed. The 4x5 was used mostly for newspapers and sports events.

It was difficult but he finally was switched over to a "120/220" Hasselblad camera that shot "Roll Film" at one tenth of the cost of the 4x5 and a very minor loss of film detail.

The main problem besides cost was that we had a hard time processing 4x5 or larger sizes of film since they were "hand processed" in what we called the "dip and dunk" system.

Film Processing System

The dip and dunk was a series of a half dozen tanks about 2 feet by 2 feet by 2 feet deep full of chemicals. The film processor had to load the sheet film into a holder in the dark after presetting the clock for the process and then by feel open the tank and drop the film in, close the tank then start the clock for the developer. Next turn the lights out, open the tank pull the film and drop into the next tank with lights out.

This continued throughout the process, only until the developing stopped in the "Stop Bath" could he turn on the lights, so he spent about 30 minutes in the dark for each run. He had to also load the 35mm and the 120mm into reels in the dark by feel and run them with the lights out.

Going one step farther, the de-facto high definition studio camera of the day was an 8x10 camera large format camera that used 8"x10" film, where a contact print could be used anywhere you needed a standard book cover size print. The 8x10 was also used by photographers like Ansel Adams for scenic shots. Where the 4x5 has 20 square inches of picture area, the 8x10 has 80 square inches or 4 times the area to capture a scene, but at over 4 times the cost of each exposure. My advice: learn how to shoot with small format before going to the cost of a large format camera.

The 16mm Sound Transfer Process

Both the Nagra (1/4 inch recording) and the Magna Sync would be "locked" to the 60 cycle "mains" (European word for electric company power line) during transfer so that the speed would be a perfect copy for lip sync from the film camera pilot tone to the final film print.

Note: My equipment was a Nagra III recorder and the microphones used were an old EV Dynamic wired lavaliere and an Electro Voice 642 shotgun mike that would have wind "pops" outdoors even when using a wind sock. The wind would move the diaphragm in the mike and produce "pops".

The EV642 was awarded an Academy Award because it was a unique design for a long distance boom or mounted mike. The mike also had a "roll off" switch to allow low end response selections. It was used a lot for boom work, which is the way I started in TV, being a "Boom Operator".

The "Pops" ruined many of the shots, but we used sound cutaways or erase pops if they fell between words. This was before decent quality lavaliere mikes (Lav's). It works best if inside a studio, but if outside the pops even with a wind sock will make you crazy.

History of Double System Sound for Movies

I watched so many films, that I could tell if sync got off only **one frame** (1/24 th of a second) while a neophyte film watcher would only notice if the sync got off maybe 3 frames or more, so the technical aspects of shooting in "sync" were paramount.

Early 16mm sound cameras like the Arri 16M recorded the magnetic sound track on the side of the "striped" 16mm film stock.

A problem was that the quality and size of the magnetic strip on the film stock produced low quality sound by having reduced audio frequency response. One other problem with Mag Stripe film is the Stripe is located on the side where the second perforations would be, but most high quality cameras use double Perf film stock for quality.

If you had Mag stripe film you needed a balancing strip on the Perf side because of the need for the film to lay flat for corner to corner focus.

Double system sound the sound had to be laid off from the Nagra III onto a full coat 16mm magnetic film for editing in a "multi gang synchronizer".

Editing Magnetic Stripe film was a pain because the camera "aperture" and the "record head" were a few inches apart, so if you cut the film straight across you could chop off the sound track. The film stock with a magnetic strip had limited optical exposure quality too as having only one perforation side the film tended to wobble in the aperture and would produce movement.

Our films were shot at 24 frames per second (Film Sound Speed) whether it was outside in the sun or inside under lights. The shooting conditions required changing the optical stock and filters to match the conditions.

Using other cameras with variable speeds we could shoot to slow the action or to speed up the action if the lighting allowed.

Now days with video tape, the sound and the pictures are recorded on the same medium interlaced between picture frames and cannot become "un-synced". Unless you change the "path link" distance for the audio, like mistakes you sometimes see on live TV. Time to bounce of a satellite is noticed on live news feeds from over seas.

Film Stock

We normally used Kodak Ektachrome reversal 7252 and 7241 Film stocks that could be "pushed" if needed to correct a shooting error. This came in handy if you knew your exposure would produce a under exposed picture because of limited light. Reversal film also was less expensive to shoot, saving the step of printing to reversal at the lab if negative was used.

Pushing Film

You would write on the can that you sent to be developed to "push" the development or extend normal processing to allow for under exposure. The lab could correct +1 or -1 stop without much problem. What the lab did was to adjust the speed the film went through the processing machine. Trying this with consumer processing they would laugh at the request.

Film – ECO 7252 EI 25

Was a color reversal low contrast film and was discontinued in 1985 and I'm sure it would be almost useless today as it was very slow, an ASA 25 for tungsten and only 16 for daylight with an 85 filter. It was a really nice alternative to negative in that handling it on a cutting bench wouldn't give you the problems of white dirt appearing on the prints.

Burn in titles were very easy and what I really liked about it was that you could shoot the stuff and do a rough cut on a bench with a jeweler's loop and thus save a nice bit of money on "work printing". It was a lovely low contrast original that gave you pretty pastel blues and greens in the prints and deep reds and yellows, especially on clear afternoons just before sunset.

Magic hour looked really magical. Grain was almost non existent, just subtle enough to look natural.

Film – EF 7241 EI 160

7241 was used for indoor shooting under Tungsten and in Daylight with the appropriate filter. It has high resolving power. The primary application is color news photography, but it can be used equally well for nighttime sporting events, for industrial photography with existing light, and for high-speed photography both by daylight and by artificial light.

The processed original camera film is ready for projection, and because it is balanced for projection at 5400 K, it is suitable for television broadcast as well.

Film – VNF 7240 EI 400

VNF replaced EF 7241 for low light. VNF or Video News Film had an incredible speed of 400, so the use of fewer and less power hungry lighting schemes this was a great thing when the reporter is toting a camera and not needing so much lighting for on scene shots.

For both VNF and Video tape the use of an "on camera" light with a working distance of 6 feet was all that was needed for an interview.

VNF was the last of it's kind of film for the News Room, as the messy film developing tanks and smells gave way to the 3/4 inch electronic VCR, which did not take the extra hours of processing needed to go from shooting footage to broadcast studio.

This paradigm shift to video tape also spelled the end of the TV studio control room 16mm film chain and it's loading of film through all the sprockets and film gates.

Cost of raw film stock and processing was the great downfall of film and archiving would take a lot of room. With videos cost savings it was a no question that evolution to video would take place.

Now with digital hard drives, storage costs less than a one cent for 10 minuets of storage, and you find the archive you want in seconds. Where film costs were $50 for 3 minuets and video was $.03 for 3 minuets the cost savings were enormous.

The Telecine or Film Chain

The film chain was a device used mostly in TV studios and control rooms. The film projectors used in a film chain are **not standard**. A special five-blade shutter, instead of the standard three bladed shutter, is used to convert the film's 24 frames per second into NTSC's 30 frame per second video.

If this was not used the video would have major flicker problems. This process is called a "3:2" pull down. Modern telecines use the same process, but it is done electronically not with a five-blade shutter. "3:2" pull down is used to convert the 24 frames per second to 30 frames per second. A normal projector has a 2 bladed shutter that shows the same frame twice.

All film projectors use sprocketed rollers to move the film and pull-down claws to move and stop the film in the gate. The film is moved in the gate when the shutter blocks the light, then the shutter is opened and the still frame is transferred to the video camera or the screen. Then the shutter is closed and the film moves to the next frame, this is repeated for each frame. If you look at a film projector a noticeable film "jitter" of the film above and below the gate, but the sprockets drives before and after the gate is moving in a continuous motion. The "loop" on either side of the gate is where the continuous movement changes to a stutter type movement so the projector gate pull down claws can stop the film when the shutter opens.

Specifications for Airborne Video

Equipment

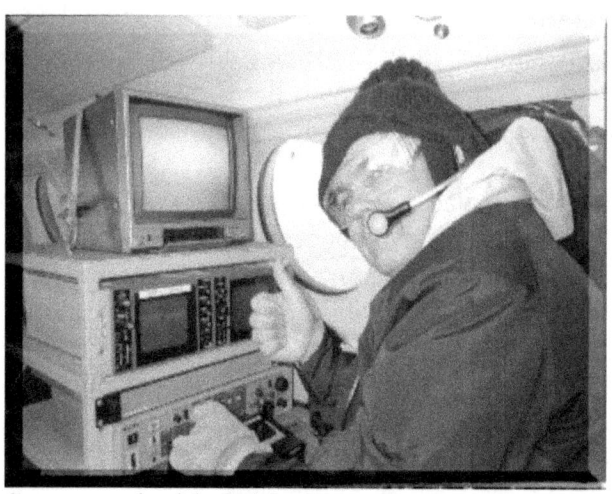

Setup used with Cabin Door Removed.

I have on "safety glasses" to keep wind borne dirt from my eyes and keep my contact lenses from freezing to my eye or drying out at high altitude. The cabin temperatures could reach -10 degrees at around 15,000 feet, the highest we can fly without oxygen and the wind is near 200 miles an hour.

On a King Air photo shoot, even with the cabin heat turned all the way up when the cabin door is removed, you still have to dress up as though you are heading to the arctic.

With ground air temperature at a comfortable 75 degrees, at altitude the outside temperature could be < 0 degrees and then coupled wind at 200 MPH the wind chill would drop past minus 40 degrees.

Just below my hands are twin "Joy Sticks" for lens control and for moving the Pan and Tilt unit left and right. Between the CCU and the Pan Tilt controls I could adjust all parameters of the camera which would include, point left right up and down, focus, zoom and expose while watching the monitors.

I also used the ships intercom to talk to the pilot and to the "subject planes". When shooting I would place the recorder in record and let it go for an hour, shoot everything and then edit what we wanted when we got back home. The Pan/Tilt control unit is for zoom, focus, pan, tilt in addition to focus and is located on the table just below my left hand.

The Camera Control unit for color, setup, gain and video level is located on the vertical rack just behind my left hand. It is usually installed in a production control room, and allows various aspects of the video camera on the studio floor to be controlled remotely.

The most commonly made adjustments are for white balance and aperture / Lens F Stop, although almost all technical adjustments are made from controls on the CCU rather than on the camera.

Above the Camera control unit is the waveform monitor, just below television monitor, a special type of oscilloscope used in television applications. The level of a video signal usually corresponds to the brightness, or luminance, of the part of the image being drawn onto a regular video screen at the same point in time.

A waveform monitor can be used to display the overall brightness of a television picture. It can also be used to visualize and observe special signals in the vertical blanking interval of a video signal, as well as the color burst between each line of video.

Below and next to my legs are two power units, one for 12 Volts DC to run the recorder. Also located next to the 12 volt supply is a 115Volt 60 Cycle AC system to run the Monitor, CCU, Vector scope and the Pan/Tilt system.

Also located on the P/T table is the intercom / com radio system so that I can transmit to my pilot and the other planes.

Sony DXC-750 2/3" 3 Chip Power HAD – Camera

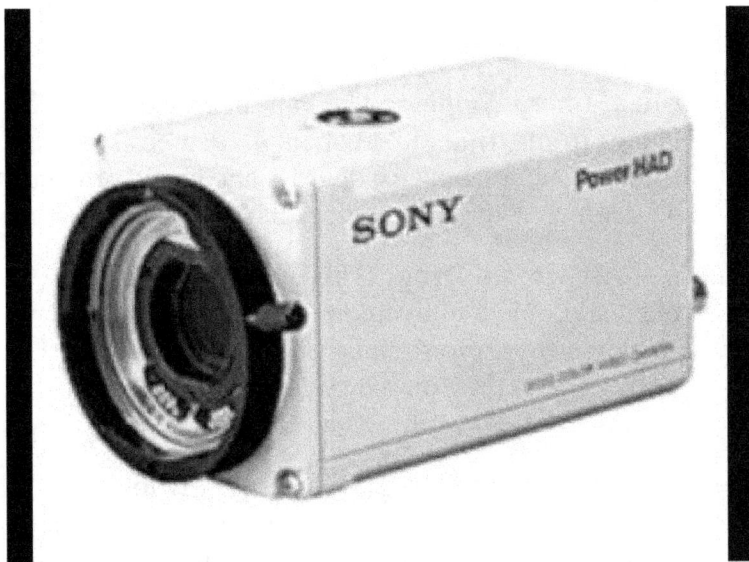

Sony DXC-750 2/3" 3 Chip Power HAD is a High Resolution NTSC camera head. This camera was later replaced with a **DXC-755** because of the size of the cable the "750" needed to "drag" around the faring built for the Telemetric's Pan Tilt system below.

Outside Pan Tilt Hanging from Belly of Aircraft

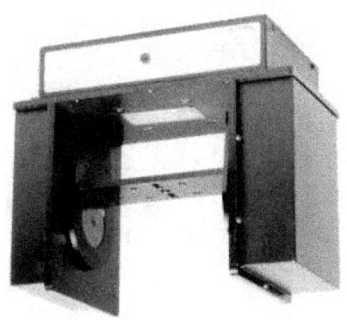

The Telemetric's Pan Tilt system was upgraded from the original "Parallel" system to a "Serial" system that uses a smaller cable and delivered the same results.

The camera fits on the platform between the larger vertical pieces. The entire unit would hang under the fuselage about even with the back cabin door.

Camera Angles: The Pan tilt would allow angles from "dead aft" to about 45 degrees left or right and up to about 10 degrees above and down to 45 degrees without drag vibration problems.

Air stream Drag: This is amounted to the biggest problem to overcome. As I rotated the camera away from straight "aft" to any other direction, the drag on the system would increase until the camera would go no farther.

Overcoming Drag: The only way to rotate the camera to "forward" would be to ask my pilot to reduce speed to "Maneuvering" at which time I could rotate to forward position because of lower airspeed and drag. This is where a beefed up pan tilt unit with its higher power could overcome the drag.

Video Formats

PAL SECAM

PAL / SECAM and other 25 frames per systems the film projector is speeded up one frame per second, to 25 frame/s. This gives a one-to-one film to video frame transfer ratio. On this system a standard 2 bladed shutter can be used. Pal is used in Europe while SECAM is used in France only.

I would go to Hollywood's Image Transform in North Hollywood to oversee the transfer from film master to a master video tape using Rank Cintel Mark III flying spot scanner (often called a Telecine).

As it paved the way for a shift from projector based transfer to a more gentle system that allowed the easy transfer of positive or negative film.

Now I hear you saying, why are you going back to film master and not just stick with straight video?

The answer is, sometimes you had to shoot in film to get the benefits of the film in the project and then transfer to video for distribution. This gave you the benefits of a "film look" on a video tape product.

The cost of distribution in film was over $150 per print while the same look on video would be $1.50. Also a factor was storage space, if you needed 100 films for distribution the space required to store the film was say 60 square feet while VHS was 12 square feet for the blanks to be made on demand.

I would like to thank the following for their contribution to this book.

Karl Berg, Robert D. Braddy, Doug Ambler, Mike Barnes, Ken Freeman, John Cook, Jim Zluticky, Guy Kassel, Rex Allen, Cliff Robertson, J. Douglas Allen, Rick Heeb, Paul Bowen, Ken Widger, Clay Lacy.

Roger Stevens, Merle Larue, Jim Yarnell, Steve Millham, Steve Sayre, Charles Kanaga, Burt Rutan, Linden Blue, Mike Potts, Tony Marlow, Dennis Hilgerson , Mike Preston, Bud Francis, Tom Carr, Bob Newsom, Jim Dolby, Hal Needham, Bob Nettmann, Rob Poe, Ron Bowering and many more.

Link to Films and Videos Discussed in this Book

Traveling to other parts of the world, taking part in historic events and meeting a bunch of great people; there is no question **I would do it again.**

- Econohost Support Site
- How to Buy Cheap Airline Tickets
- How to Make Good Photos